Administration: Principles, Theory and Practice

Administration: Principles, Theory and Practice

With Applications to Physical Education

J. TILLMAN HALL *University of Southern California*

JOHN M. COOPER *Indiana University*

REUBEN B. FROST *Springfield College*

HENRY SHENK *University of Kansas*

NED WARREN *Eastern Kentucky University*

ROGER C. WILEY *Washington State University*

GOODYEAR PUBLISHING COMPANY, INC.
Pacific Palisades, California

Library of Congress Catalog Card Number:
73-83393

ISBN: 0-87620-018-8
Y-0188-6

Current Printing (Last Number):
10 9 8 7 6 5 4 3 2 1

Printed in the United States of America

Dedicated to
the memory of a very lovely lady
Lenore C. Smith, Ph.D.

Preface

This book presents the fundamental issues in administration, concentrating on administration in the colleges. While primarily concerned with topics appropriate to almost any kind of administrative endeavor, we draw on our experiences in college physical education departments.

There are six chapters; each is written by an expert in his field and each is a separate entity. The authors were selected because they all have had long, successful tenures as administrators. Each author lives in a different region, and therefore, the book reflects administrative practices throughout the United States.

The six authors had several face-to-face conferences where ideas were exchanged so that each chapter incorporates the thinking of more than just its author. A distinct topic is covered in each chapter, but on occasion, there is overlapping of subject matter. We decided to leave this slight repetition rather than to interfere with the organization of the topics.

The book differs from others on administration in that we focus on the management of personnel rather than on the handling of equipment and facilities. People make things happen, and the management of people is a complex matter. The administrator must be an innovator, a stimulator, and an evaluator. We believe that our book aids him in his challenging tasks.

Throughout, the authors recommend techniques that stimulate faculty members to exert themselves for their departments. Recommendations include the following: join a cause larger than your own personal interest; bring out the best in one another; never settle for second if first is available; everyone should be a trouble shooter.

The authors wish to express their special appreciation to all their colleagues and students for their ideas, recommendations, and support in all of their innovative administrative endeavors. An administrator cannot be happy or successful unless the faculty and students believe in the course that he has charted. Therefore, we thank you for giving us the opportunity to serve you.

TILLMAN HALL

Contents

chapter 1   # Principles, Policies, and Theories of Administration

J. TILLMAN HALL

This chapter examines the wide range of principles, policies, and theories used in administration of all kinds and emphasizes how these theories operate in administering health, physical education, and recreation programs. To be effective, an administrator needs to be both knowledgeable about his field and convinced that it is vital.

We begin, then, with the contributions that physical education has made to civilization. Scholars believe that it is a bulwark against man's deficiencies. Major qualities developed in a good physical education program are stamina, endurance, coordination, strength, and good posture. In this age of industrialization, urbanization, and automation, programs for the development of these qualities at all ages are essential; otherwise, man may not survive. Lately, society has increasingly demonstrated concern for the optimum development and maintenance of the body. These responsibilities have become the major thrust of teachers of physical education.

Dedicated to his chosen field, the administrator can turn his attention to principles, policies, and theories.

TERMS

Administration

As used in this book, refers to the management of all departmental affairs. It includes the management of facilities, purchase and care of equipment, the supervision of personnel, along with the complete development of the physical education program.

Mode of Operations

Administrative effectiveness frequently hinges on the development of an acceptable manual or code of operations through which the objectives and policies of the department are defined, along with the duties and responsibilities of all departmental personnel. This manual should be the product of a departmental study and should be continuously updated to include agreed-upon operational procedures. In essence, it explains how departmental decisions are and will be made.

This code of operations should include a divisional and unit conspectus with recommended implementation procedures. Favorable faculty responsiveness to departmental rules and regulations is closely related to the degree in which the faculty is involved in their formation. The faculty should have a voice in determining who is responsible for various departmental details, how changes may occur, and how decisions are made and implemented.

Principles

Usually defined as a general truth derived from the accumulation, classification, examination, verification, evaluation, experimentation, and observation of specific circumstances. In administration, principles imply integrity, uprightness, and standard rules of conduct. In general, they are temporal and have normative priority. The principles of physical education come from the sciences of anatomy, anthropology, biology, embryology, gerontology, physiology, psychology, and sociology. We have synthesized many of our fundamental disciplinary beliefs from the body of knowledge provided by these subjects.

The principles of administration are based upon the subject areas dealing with business education, municipal and school administration, social psychology, and business management. In a broad sense, these disciplines have concerned themselves with individual differences. It is at this point, administration becomes most challenging. Management tenets consist of axioms determined by conventional precepts. Administrative principles should be specifically selected to convey the greatest good for the largest number. This selection always should imply ethical procedures; truth is not easily found if operational procedures are influenced by biases and prejudices. Principles without validity do not usually connote truth. There is an old adage, "Nothing can be right in practice if it is wrong in principle," which describes the concepts recommended in selecting the principles of administration. The principles one selects in administration usually reflect one's own personal value concepts.

The term *value* in a sense used as a synonym for "worth" or "goodness," is ambiguous, often possessing abstract and concrete, objective and subjective qualities. Value is placed on something as the result of judgment and involves both extrinsic and intrinsic qualities.

The selection of administrative principles should be based on knowledge, experience, good judgment, discretion, and sagacity. Those in administration need all the wisdom they can muster in making the correct decisions. Sound administration requires the adherence to sound principles.

Policy

Primarily this term refers to courses of action, seldom to permanent principles. Administrative policies are usually generalizations about organizational behavior. Statements about departmental policy may be either prospective or retrospective. In the latter case, policy refers to a principle determined in the past. Prospective policy statements refer to actions expected to take place.

Administrative policies are derived from principles and rules selected to guide a department toward specific objectives. These objectives are determined by the faculty, the school, the profession, social mores, and public opinion. They should reflect accepted practices of the time and place.

INNOVATIVE ADMINISTRATION

Fundamental changes are required to deal with the new world we are entering. Some say the culture within which we live was designed for an earlier period when man was trying to increase his power rather than share it with his colleagues. Currently, there is overwhelming evidence that a huge amount of new knowledge has been released in a relatively short period of time. However, in a sense this vast information is still in code; little has been translated or converted to purposeful use, workable procedures, or teachable language.

The administrator must learn to decipher research and pull from it findings that advance theory and practice. This process is not as easy as it sounds, because he continuously deals with colliding forces that stimulate questions for which society has not found any popular answers. Furthermore, many administrators in the inner circle appear to have a decreasing commitment to past policies. Along with these changes, administrators are occasionally bombarded with abrasive problems from dissident groups who protest against the establishment. The essence of good innovative leadership seems to be to know when to ignore opinion, when to accede to it, and when to try to marshal it. Frequently, this type of leadership is labeled unimaginative; because it never appears to be much ahead of public opinion, people think it is rather fuzzy.

Innovation means more than something new; it frequently requires casting off outdated ideologies, nostalgic practices, and assumptions about mainstream policies.

The wheel of time seems to have spun full circle—once again it is popular to ask questions and challenge all practices. The tide is running against tradition; extremism, in the defense of what is right, is no vice, and moderation is not considered a virtue. Today, expressed convictions are immediately challenged by someone; perhaps that is the way things should be. However, because quality research seems to reveal that the finding of *truth* is not easy, an increasing number of administrators are a little unsteady and unsure of themselves. They seem to be less desirous of making hard and unpopular decisions than they were a few years ago. This reluctance may be due to the fact that, after a change sets in motion some consequences, painful introspection occurs.

Lately, schools that use data processing seem to be taking on the atmosphere of business and are losing the atmosphere of a place of learning. Archaic procedures in the management of education can no longer be tolerated. Moods of uncertainty must be expelled because the time for fresh thinking is long overdue.

The administrator is responsible for developing the teamwork essential in building a dynamic physical education department. He is responsible for punching the keys that make students and faculty feel like partners. The innovative administrator discovers a way to inspire confidence. He possesses exceptional awareness, identifies and articulates the major issues, assimilates and distributes pertinent information, advocates moral guidelines, and defends ethics.

The administrator moves in many circles and plays a variety of roles. His imagination, competitiveness, charisma, along with a host of similar attributes, are important in ways not easily observable. His functions include gathering information, initiating activity, elaborating on ideas, encouraging and supporting creativity, setting standards, and conducting meetings, and synthesizing and expressing group opinions. Perhaps his first and most important function should be to gain and to maintain the confidence of his colleagues. Without their support, very little is likely to happen.

FIRST IMPRESSIONS

The director must be cognizant of the many factors which create that important first impression. Cleanliness and tidiness of person, office, and surroundings, along with attentiveness and ability to speak fluently, generally make the first meeting rewarding. Other attributes just as important are ability to listen, open mindedness, appropriate manners and courtesies. Logical procedures tempered with sincere warmth and friendliness usually impress almost anyone.

Appropriate packaging of these attributes coupled with adequate knowledge usually gets the administrator under way in good order. The absence of any one of these qualities may prevent faculty-student support and bring about ineffective relationships. Leadership is both an art and a science. The administrator learns from science what is right to do. Then he must exercise his art and go about doing it in the right way.

THEORY

This word has various meanings and is often contrasted with "practice" and "unverified speculation." Some use it to signify a hypothesis, whether confirmed or not. Usually, in administration, it refers to a system of relationships advanced as the explanation of observed events. It frequently falls short of conclusive demonstration, yet implies sufficient evidence to bestow plausibility. Administration, like most other academic fields of study, supports numerous rival theories. These conflicting theories perhaps exist because each administrator prefers a particular set of values, principles, objectives, or procedures. Just as there may be many roads to the top of a mountain, there may be several equally applicable theories of administration. It is generally believed that theory precedes practice by some twenty to fifty years.

It may be advantageous to specifically identify one's value concepts before adopting a particular theory. Some say one should first choose the theory, others that this places the cart before the horse. The important task is to select the most effective way to do something. Above all else, the administrator must pursue truth, honesty, integrity, professional ethics, and efficiency—or what is education all about?

Oftentimes people are thrust into administration without first having had an opportunity to prepare adequately for multidimensional responsibilities. In fact, too many physical education administrators have had inadequate academic administrative preparation before they become head of a department. In their work, they have given very little attention—and that has not been effective—to selecting compatible principles; they have almost no practice in establishing acceptable policies or in analyzing prospective administrative procedures. They have learned on the job, thus diminishing early administrative effectiveness.

Because of these short-sighted practices, many worthy projects and potentially good administrators are doomed to failure. In order to avoid needless opposition to selected procedures, countless related and very influential factors and circumstances—such as existing school policies, faculty and student sentiments, along with the administrator's own personality—must blend into a harmonious whole. If the administrator's personality is not in concert with an adopted theory, unavoidable discords are bound to occur. An administrator's effectiveness is definitely related to the theory's compatibility with those it serves.

All of this process may sound easy to come by, but one must keep in mind the innumerable, inescapable demands made on the administrator. There never seems to be enough time to adequately study all those areas for which he is responsible. The confusion between faculty and student values, the crunch of events, the difficulties of working with tempestuous people, the attempts to move past formidable barriers—all tend to prevent him from making quick and orderly decisions. Yet policy formation and decision-making are among his major responsibilities. Frequently, his work appears to be an exercise in futility, especially if he is forced to work with a faculty member who refuses to compromise or agree in principle with anything, who possesses an indignant attitude, believing he has a corner on knowledge, and who seems to detest the very thought of cooperation.

Individuals like this occasionally create a logjam of opposition to what might appear to be rather routine problems. Therefore, it behooves the administrator to develop systematic, deliberate plans that stimulate rational behavior. Furthermore, he must develop ways to work efficiently with those below and above his observation post. At no time can he assume that, if he deals solely with the whales, the minnows will tag along. Because of the time involved, many professional administrators dislike rap sessions about symbolism—this is particularly true if they have been there before. But the "mind-set" administrator is rapidly becoming a thing of the past; he can no longer escape to his privileged sanctuary or mark time by standing pat. He must develop a viable, unobstructed view of how the department can move toward meaningful goals with a reasonable chance of being successful. The theory he subscribes to should provide constructive recommendations on how to obtain the cooperation of the faculty, students, alumni, and other interested parties.

Clear research is not yet available on many of the newer theories of administration. This lack is particularly true in physical education, and has created considerable pervasive nervousness. Despite all the research in education, no revolutionary potpourri of ideas has come forth. Much of what has been said about the newer theories of administration is in the nature of hypothesis. Automation, computation, simulation, and all the other potentials of modern cybernetics have scarcely been used in physical education. Modern sophisticated techniques seem to be as muscle-bound as the archaic stereotyped view of the overdeveloped physique.

Although too many physical education departments appear to be repositories of old methods, course outlines, and superannuated trivia, they have avoided change for change's sake—which could have been equally detrimental. Everyone knows it is easier to recognize an error than to find truth. But we must be aware that numerous new concepts are struggling to be born. The dynamic, forward-looking administrator can no longer afford to take the horse nearest the stable door. The profession needs some research of its own that can be utilized. Without research, there is no evidence; without evidence, there is no reason to change. Until valid research has been done, critical introspection and/or educated guesses will dictate most changes.

Major Theories of Administration

Minimal attention has been given in physical education books to this topic. Theories are usually related to types of administrators and types of leadership; some authorities refer to methods and characteristics of leaders. But for some unknown reason, writers in the field of physical education avoid the word *theory* as if it were an unmanageable term. They seem to understand the meaning of the word, but prefer a different term. Yet the word *theory* is the most conclusive and descriptive for the ideas relating to how one administers a department.

Based upon observation, experience, and numerous references, it appears to this author that a majority of physical education administrators inadvertently favors one of the following major theories: autocratic, aristocratic, democratic, laissez-faire, and eclectic. Each theory may be viewed as a systematic statement of principles and methods; the autocratic and the laissez-faire theories are at the two extremes of a continuum. An analysis of each of the alleged theories tends to reveal the following salient characteristics:

Autocratic Theory. In its broadest sense, refers to a system in which authority comes from above without the consent of those governed. This authority can be exercised by a force or persuasion, or by a combination of both. The system is considered undemocratic because it is independent of the will of the governed. The smaller the department, the stronger are its authoritarian tendencies; in a two- or three-member department, such characteristics are most clearly discernible. The administrator does not allow the faculty to govern itself through chosen representatives or to use their own judgment in making fundamental decisions. Different types of administrative functions may be distinguished under the autocratic theory. So-called line-staff functions are generally concerned with achieving ends that the given authority has established. Certain auxiliary functions have to do with organization, personnel, material, finance, and planning, which are necessary to the operation of the department. An administrator adhering to this theory is most likely to be arbitrary, inconsiderate, coercive, and to employ tight, inflexible controls over his faculty and his department.

This theory is rarely successful in departmental administration in a democratic society. Cues of discontentment may be observed in resentment and in the lack of initiative, enthusiasm, and morale. Furthermore, the staff turnover is usually quite high.

Aristocratic Theory. In general, the rule of the best few—the morally and intellectually superior govern the rest of the department. Even though many physical education administrators would deny they are adhering to this practice, it is more prevalent than one generally surmises. In a more practical sense, we refer to the department managed by the upper layer of the faculty as aristocratic. Contrary to popular opinion, these people tend to be the innovators in the department. Perhaps they do represent the most learned, imaginative and creative members of the faculty; it is well known that they are the best paid.

Under this theory of administration, there is always a tendency for this upper layer to end up with the best teaching assignments, hold the most important departmental chairmanships, be the first to obtain promotions, receive the largest pay increases, have more privileges, and get the most prestigious and influential positions.

Followers of this theory tend to believe that certain faculty members are better educated, more dedicated, and exercise better judgment concerning the department's prosperity.

Democratic Theory. Most administrators claim they believe in this theory, which advocates the greatest good for the greatest number. In the strictest sense, the theory refers to rule by the majority. Another historic way of defining it is that a department of faculty and students should be managed by the faculty and students for the faculty and students. Administrators who adhere to this theory proclaim a doctrine of human rights in which all freedoms, privileges, and opportunities should be equal.

This theory recognizes the inner dignity of all those involved in the educational process. It implies that the majority shall decide among issues. There is freedom of speech, press, and religion. Furthermore, everyone has the right to oppose, in a peaceful manner, any departmental policy or practice that he dislikes. Basically, this theory stands for a method of administration rather than a set of rules. Administrators pursuing this practice encourage the faculty to become involved in departmental affairs.

Occasionally, when practiced, the democratic theory does slow down progress. However, in the final analysis, the majority gains in many ways. This is true of education in a democracy.

Laissez-faire Theory. Defined as minimum interference or control over others' actions. Favoring individualism, it assumes that each of us is the best judge of his or her own welfare. Furthermore, it implies that no artificial barriers should interfere with the individual's initiative. The doctrine of individualism is at the opposite end of the continuum from collectivism.

Proponents of this theory believe that the individual is most productive when he pursues his own self-interests without external restrictions. The administrator generally doubting that there is one superior strategy, as far as possible encourages faculty members to choose their own methodology.

Eclectic Theory. When one chooses selected ideas, values, principles, and procedures from different theories, he is called an eclectic. Some use the term *situational theory*. I suspect that this practice most accurately describes the present-day philosophy of many physical education administrators. Most of them probably attempt to take the best from all they know and, without a doubt, this practice has been the strength of the theory.

Its major disadvantages seem to come about when various conflicting principles are selected, melted, and compressed into practice. Those adhering to this theory have occasionally been confronted by faculty unrest because of opposing value judgments. Stereotyped procedures in solving these conflicts have seldom been successful. If, through imaginative inventiveness, one could overcome these procedural difficulties, the other inconsistent elements of the theory might be ascertained.

The theory does permit one to utilize research findings without destroying the entire administrative framework. If there were no other inherent values in the eclectic theory, this one alone appears to be very substantial.

Other Theories of Administration

A number of additional theories, some situational in nature, have gained popularity, particularly in other areas of administration. In general, these theories relate to the business world; however, occasionally, they tend to describe the situational practice for physical education. A brief description of six theories follows.

Classical Organizational Theory. Infused within this theory is the belief that there are many fundamental and universal truths. This statement indicates the theory's relationship to traditional idealistic philosophy. In many respects, the classical theory resembles the autocratic, particularly in line-staff functions and responsibilities. It tends to be opposite present trends; it is supportive of the generalist rather than the specialist. Furthermore, it contains antidemocratic bias which in essence has a dehumanizing effect on the faculty.

Some additional limitations of this theory are: its assumptions about motivations are inaccurate; it does not solve conflicts of interest; it gives individualism minimal consideration; it pays sparse attention to the role of cognition in problem solving.

Empirical Theory. This theory resembles both the classical organizational and the autocratic theories in many respects. The theory states that administration, unlike law, should not be bound by precedent; situations and conditions of the future are not likely to be similar to those of the past. In essence, it is a case study approach.

Human Behavior Theory. Deliberately concentrating on the people part of administration, this theory tends to deal more specifically with interpersonal relationships. It stresses group dynamics with special emphasis on goals, purposes, and rational behavior. More specifically, it is oriented toward social psychology, which should also be a concern for those in administration. Scholars whose major belief lies in this theory seem to place primary focus on the individual as a sociopsychological being and what is required to motivate him. Some critics imply that its major focus is too much on good leadership and not enough on good managership.

Social Systems Theory. Closely related to the human behavior theory with specific emphasis on interpersonal relationships, this theory is sociological in nature and subject to all the pressures and conflicts of the cultural environment. Understanding group dynamics is one, but not the only, important phase of managing a department.

Decision Theory. Concerned with the rational behavior approach to decision making, advocates of this theory give special consideration to a large number of social and psychological problems as possible alternatives in the decision-making process. Not only are they concerned with evaluating alternatives, but with a broad view of the possible needed changes in the entire social system.

Mathematical Theory. Relates to models and processes along with the use of symbols for unknown data. Other distinguishing characteristics of the theory are orderly thinking, quantitative measurements, and logical processes. This day and time, few would find fault with the mathematical approach to any field of inquiry. However, it could be dangerous to assume that the thousands of details one is confronted with in administration could be reduced to a mathematical formula. Nevertheless, many aspects of this theory should be utilized more than they have been if administration is to gain in respectability.

Summary. In summary, the author recognizes the confusion generally observed in management theory. A comprehensive understanding of any one theory requires extensive study. In fact, an entire book could be written about each.

This skeletal definition of the various theories has been presented as a springboard for student discussion and for later extensive student research related to management theory.

In the following chapter, "Administrative Patterns," Dr. Wiley takes the discussion a step further and relates it more specifically to the patterns observed in the administration of physical education departments.

BIBLIOGRAPHY

Bucher, Charles A. *Administrative Dimensions of Health and Physical Education Programs, Including Athletics.* St. Louis: The C. V. Mosby Company, 1971.

Daughtrey, Greyson, and Woods, John B. *Physical Education Programs: Organization and Administration.* Philadelphia: W. B. Saunders Company, 1971.

Dennis, James Mercer. "Administrative Behavior of Successful and Unsuccessful Athletic Directors in Small Colleges and Universities." PhD. dissertation, University of Southern California, 1971.

Golembiewski, Robert T. *Organizing Men and Power.* Chicago: Rand, McNally, and Company, 1967.

Hall, J. Tillman. *School Recreation: Its Organization, Supervision, and Administration.* Dubuque: Wm. C. Brown and Company, 1966.

Havel, Richard C., and Seymour, Emery W. *Administration of Health, Physical Education and Recreation for Schools.* New York: The Ronald Press Company, 1961.

Katz, Daniel and Kahn, Robert L. *The Social Psychology of Organizations.* New York: John Wiley and Sons, 1966.

March, James G. and Simon, Herbert A. *Organizations.* New York: John Wiley and Sons, 1958.

Miller, David W. and Starr, Martin K. *The Structure of Human Decisions.* Englewood Cliffs, N.J.: Prentice-Hall, 1967.

Pfiffner, John M. and Sherwood, Frank P. *Administrative Organization.* Englewood Cliffs, N.J.: Prentice-Hall, 1960.

Voltmer, Edward F. and Esslinger, Arthur A. *The Organization and Administration of Physical Education.* New York: Appleton-Century-Crofts, 1967.

Wadia, Maneck S. *The Nature and Scope of Management.* California Western University: Scott, Foresman, and Company, 1966.

Williams, Jesse Fering. *The Principles of Physical Education.* Philadelphia: W. B. Saunders Company, 1948.

chapter 2   Administrative Patterns

ROGER C. WILEY

The organizational patterning of colleges and universities in the United States has evolved over a period of years under a variety of forces and influences. The tradition of self-goverment, which is so essential to the American university, has existed in European colleges and universities since the Middle Ages; however, there has been considerable change in how these institutions organize their faculties and administrations.

Harvard became the first and leading exponent of the bicameral system of administration in the higher education institution. It used a bipartite form of government, with clergy, magistrates, and the president forming one group and the president, treasurer, and faculty forming the other, a resident group. Yale was responsible for establishing the unicameral form of government. A single governing board, on which the founders of Yale held all the seats, proved to be a new model for America.

More recent evolution of the administrative patterning demonstrates the influence of the German concept wherein the graduate and professional schools are grafted to the basic liberal arts. Then came the addition of formerly independent faculties in such fields as medicine, pharmacy, and law. Exploding enrollments and burgeoning demands made on the university forced boards of regents to seek new ways to organize the faculties and programs for more efficient administration. Additional pressures by regional accrediting agencies have caused state agencies to examine the structures of the universities to ensure that organizational efficiency, economy of operation, and internal organization are at their best.[1]

DEVELOPMENT OF ORGANIZATIONAL PATTERNS

Over the years, very little study has been done on the structuring of colleges and universities. In the main, most of the early teachings on organizational theory were accomplished on business and industrial management by such pioneers as Mary Follett, Herbert Simon, Lyndall Urwick, Marshall Dimock, Chris Argyris, Peter Blau, W. Richard Scott, James March, Max Weber, and Chester Barnard, to name a few. As reported by Dr. Hall in Chapter 1, several schools and theories of administration have been identified and discussed. Those that seem to have made their impressions on organizational patterns in higher education are discussed below.

THEORIES OF ADMINISTRATION AND ORGANIZATION

Filley and House stated that there are two approaches to the study of management and organization—normative and positive. Classical theory, they say, is normative and prescriptive in nature; it sets forth guides for actions and activities to be performed. Design theory, which is positive, descriptive, and explanatory in nature, seeks to generalize design for all structures with disregard for goal and environmental differences.[2]

Traditional organization theory, according to Johnson, Kast, and Rosenzweig, evolved from concepts of structure, hierarchy, authority, specialization, span of control, and line and staff relationships.[3] Of more practical interest to the reader are the various models developed over the years which have been identified by Johnson, Kast, and Rosenzweig:

> 1. *Bureaucratic model:* an organization which would provide a maximum rationality in human behavior. It would contain key elements of division of labor based on functional specialization, a well-defined hierarchy of authority, a system of rules covering the rights and duties of incumbents, a system of procedures for dealing with work situations, impersonality of interpersonal relations, and promotion and selection for employment based upon technical competence.

2. *Neoclassical model:* a human relations model of organizational behavior which is based on the thesis that informal organizations grow out of social needs—the needs of people for interpersonal association with others.

3. *Professional model:* an organization in which the focus of attention is on problems of certain types in which knowledge is produced, applied, preserved, or communicated in systems especially established for these purposes. This model needs to utilize the traditional bureaucratic mechanisms for routine activities and provide a system for nonuniform events and for innovation.

4. *Decision-making model:* an organization in which the primary emphasis is placed on the human problem-solving process and decision mechanism. In this organization, participants are not merely viewed as mechanical instrumentalities but perceived as individuals with wants, motives, aspirations levels, and drives and who have limited rationality and capacity for problem solving.[4]

Two principal competing concepts of organization and administration have been identified by Morphet, Johns, and Reller. They use the terms *traditional monocratic, bureaucratic concept* and *emerging pluralistic, collegial concept* in describing extreme ends of the continuum of administration and organization. The former term is used to describe the organizational structure as a pyramidal and hierarchical model in which all power for making decisions flows from superordinates to subordinates. The emerging pluralistic, collegial concept is best described as a modification of the monocratic, bureaucratic concept. In this concept, the organization is structured hierarchically to implement programs and policy, and collegially on an egalitarian basis for making policy and program decisions. The latter best describes that which is common as a model for colleges and universities today; the former, that which identifies early industrial organizational models.[5]

Of recent vintage is the growing concept of system theory from which has evolved the Planned Program and Budgeting System (PPBS) of accountability and fiscal management. Johnson, Kast, and Rosenzweig viewed the systems concept by treating the organization as a system of mutually dependent parts and variables with attainment of the organizational goals as paramount and with coordination of the activities and identification of the subgoals as a part of the total system.[6]

CHARACTERISTICS OF ORGANIZATIONS

Even though, in recent years, most dicussions dealing with organizations have centered on the development of behavioral theory, little has been done to identify for the administrator of public schools and colleges what principles should be followed. While it is generally agreed that organizational structure should be goal oriented, little has been done to make it flexible and adaptive to innovation and change. Generally, public school and university administrators are reluctant to modify a structure to accomodate change. For that matter, so are the faculties of these systems.

Wilson identified three basic stituations that occur when consideration is given to structuring an organization:

> First, every person regardless of his level of ability and job assignment, experiences certain felt needs. . . .
> Secondly, formal relationships based upon an assignment of authority will be supplemented by informal relationships based upon group response to a natural leader. . . .
> Thirdly, there is often real or latent conflict between those in authority and others. . . .[7]

Morphet, Johns, and Reller indicate that formal organizations tend to develop pyramidal, hierarchical structures that show a head-and-tail relationship between various agents in the system.[8] Most authorities agree that as an organization grows and becomes larger and more complex, it also becomes more bureaucratic and hierarchical in its structure.

If an organization is to be strong, focus must be placed upon organizational effectiveness and not on administrative efficiency, as has been all too true in the past.

Departmentation

Departmentation is a basic characteristic of the organizational structure. The work of organizational management is specialized, with the authority and responsibility for efficient performance assigned to administrators of various ranks. Several methods are employed to achieve such specialization. Petersen, Plowman, and Trickett identified four types of primary departmentation, territorial (place), commodities (product), customer (patronage), and functional (process). For purposes of discussion and relevancy, only two, customer and functional, are discussed in this chapter.[9]

Customer Departmentation. In coeducational universities, management is familiar with the division of living halls into residential areas on the basis of sex. In business, grouping of activities according to types of patrons served is the basis on which the organization is patterned.[10]

Functional Departmentation. This type of departmentation is found in most organizations where even a rudimentary separation of activities is undertaken.* As an organization grows, it tends to subdivide many of its basic functions into tasks. Quite often, these tasks become separate departments. (Tasks denote activities somewhat specialized in character that are assigned to and performed by individuals or groups within the organization.) Quite often, grouping of activities by close association rather than by similarity of activities is the rule. Petersen, Plowman, and Trickett have suggested seven criteria for determining how such association may be realized: use, interest, segregation, suppressed competition, control, separation, and coordination.[11]

For the architect of an organization, combining activities into workable units of administration is probably one of the most difficult of organizational duties. Adopting a pattern of administration can be simplified if early attention is given to this aspect of planning.

PATHWAYS OF AUTHORITY

The optimum organizational structure, hence its pathways of authority, is determined in part by the element of communication. Hampton, Summer, and Webber point out that where problems are being met and communication is taking place, it is inevitable that a "hub" man or decision maker emerge. Hierarchy, control, and predictability, they say, are essential for organizational effectiveness.[12]

In traditional staff-line operational charts, the pathways of authority differed from level to level in the hierarchy, and from person to person within the level of the hierarchy. For the most part, staff functions were of an advisory nature and thus, only an implied threat of authority existed. While the line of authority was easy to portray in an organizational chart and while the subordinate could easily distinguish the difference between staff and line functions, sometimes informal pathways were developed. At this point organizational experts, who identified and studied these relationships, suggested that there are two types of pathways of authority that exist in modern day organizational structures—formal and informal.

---

*The major share of the information dealing with departmentation is to be credited to Elmore Petersen, E. Grosvenor Plowman, and Joseph M. Trickett whose book *Business Organization and Management* contains an excellent chapter, "Departmentation and Its Criteria."

Formal Pathways

Committees. In early classical texts on management and organization, the failure to mention committees in the building of organizations seemed in violation of these principles in the early construction of hierarchies. Sayles and Strauss conclude that committees are a fact of organizational life. They suggest that the question is not whether to permit them but when it is best to use them.[13]

Committees are a necessary way of life in most professional kinds of organizations. Without their use, the equal basis for policy making and program determination would not and could not exist. Committees function for the purpose of exchanging ideas, making policy decisions, recommending action, or generating ideas.[14] They are placed in the organizational chart at a point where they do not encroach upon the established responsibilities of the group or person to whom they are responsible. Usually small in size (five to seven members are suggested), they have a leader, and their membership contains a heterogenous sample of people from within the organization. While in corporate enterprises committees are useful in facilitating exchange of information between groups not normally having contact with one another, their use in professional groups extends well beyond an exchange of information concept. In more recent years, where boards of directors are utilized, the development of executive committees to handle many of the organization's routine business affairs has occurred.

Committees operate in much the same way as the entire organization: they set goals, plan and act, and prepare recommendations that are reported back.[15] Their use in facilitating the exchange of ideas and allowing participation in exercising the principle of shared responsibility is most important.

Chain of Command. In military establishments, the chain of command or the appropriate channel of communication is well defined. Likewise, in organizations where information is needed and decisions demanded, the route of communication should be clear and have some built-in redundancy. Short-circuiting is usually indicative of channel breakdown. While organizational charts usually show only the more formal pathways of activity, some understood rules and regulations should exist that spell out alternatives for information retrieval.

In more recent times, some organizations have utilized the position of ombudsman as a device to cut through established routes of communication.

Informal Pathways

No matter how well defined an organizational chart is, informal pathways of authority do develop. Hampton, Summer, and Webber describe what the meaning of membership in informal groups can mean to individuals within an organization. They point out that the informal group serves three functions for the individual:

1. the satisfaction of complex social needs
2. emotional support in identifying oneself and dealing with the world
3. assistance in meeting goals[16]

Within an organizational pattern it must be recognized that informal groups are going to form. The classical grapevine with its correct and incorrect interpretation of organizational events and demands will develop. Personality, ethnicity, religion, and various socioeconomic factors will tend to influence the membership of informal groups and must be taken under advisement when modeling the organization.

Some recognition of the development of informal pathways should be considered when the organization structure is formulated. Departmentation, committee function and constituency, and number of levels in the hierarchy are but a few of the considerations that demand close inspection.

CONTEMPORARY ORGANIZATIONAL MODELS

Most large organizations and public bodies have organizational work charts. These charts, while not inflexible or completely descriptive of the organization, must necessarily be developed. They assist the viewer to better understand the organization and, better yet, they assist the corporate member in identifying where he or she fits into the organization. Petersen, Plowman, and Trickett identified seven types of organizational charts: vertical, lateral, linear, outline, levels, functional, and circular.[17] Four types are described here because of their usefulness in the situations the reader will most frequently confront.

Vertical Organizational Chart

By far the most common, this chart is considered the easiest to read, the easiest to understand, and the easiest to develop. Vertical charts, however, do not always portray what they are supposed to show. Quite often, levels of the hierarchy are distorted or incompletely shown. The size of the box tends to overexpose or underexpose the value of the position. Complex relationships are missing, since the very complexity of those relationships defies description. Emphases in positions and interrelationships disappear when attempts are made to show them schematically. Most vertical charts are much better if they are kept simple in form and concise in design. Figure 1 is an example of a vertical organizational chart for a small municipal government.

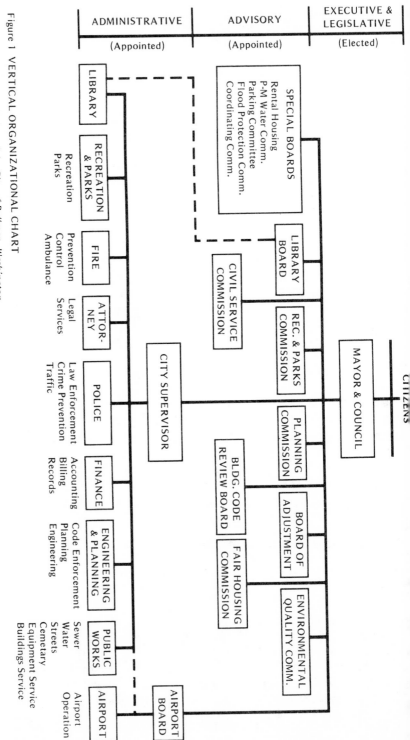

Figure 1 VERTICAL ORGANIZATIONAL CHART

Reproduced by permission of the City of Pullman, Washington

Lateral Organizational Chart

While not widely used, the lateral chart serves as a useful tool for companies wishing to show many positions not usually possible in a vertical chart. Its chief advantage is that it can show relationships without doing an injustice to the position or to the level of responsibility. As to the latter, it can group positions into a unit more easily. Since it avoids the showing of levels, which can't be accomplished in a vertical-hierarchical chart, it can include many more positions. Figure 2 is an example of a business organization utilizing a lateral chart scheme.

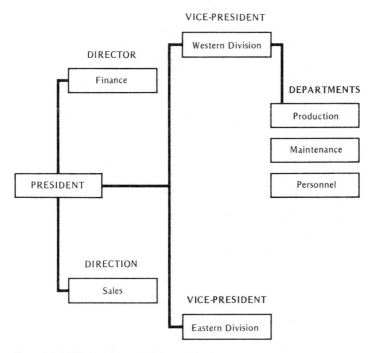

Figure 2 LATERAL ORGANIZATIONAL CHART

Linear Organizational Chart

This chart is apt to find its use in standard-operating-procedure (SOP) manuals of companies or organizations. It can be prepared by office personnel quite easily and is flexible enough so that it can be readily modified by the designer when changes occur in the structure. This chart is not commonly used; thus its usefulness is not generally known. Figure 3 is an example of a community college administrative organization utilizing a linear chart concept.

PRESIDENT-JEANETTE POORE

Dean of Instruction-Charles Skinner

INSTRUCTION

Division of Arts-Chairman: Paul H. Giroux

Division of Business Administration-Chairman: George Melton

Division of Communications-Chairman

Division of Life Sciences-Chairman: Thayne Parks

Division of Nursing-Chairman: Jean Irving

Division of Physical Education-Chairman: Dolly Holland

Division of Physical Sciences-Chairman: G. Harvey Van Arkel

Division of Social Sciences-Chairman: Wil Knutsen

Division of Vocational Education-Acting Chairman:

George Herrmann

Dean of Students-William Deller

ACTIVITIES

Director of Student Activities-Edwin Puck

Director of Athletics-Marvin Cross

Registrar-Marjorie L. Nielsen

FINANCE

Director of Financial Aids-Robert Crumbaugh

Director of Food Services-Barbara Hoffman

STAFF
OFFICERS

Career Placement Counselor-Lynn Robinson

Veterans Counselor-Larry Rodgers

Information Officer-Beverly Dobson

Figure 3. LINEAR ORGANIZATION CHART
Everett Community College Organization Chart

Adapted from 1971-1972 Catalogue of Everett Community College, Washington

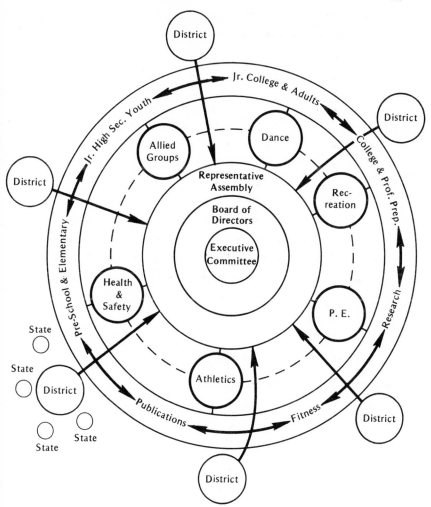

Figure 4. CIRCULAR ORGANIZATIONAL CHART
American Association for Health, Physical Education and Recreation

Reproduced with permission of the American Association for Health, Physical Education and Recreation.

Circular Organizational Chart

Circular charts display a flare for the unique, yet have a place in the organization that wishes to play down the "above and below" feeling that people get from other charts. Some claim that circular charts do a better job of showing positional relationships and presenting a picture of a tightly unified body. They do provide the reader with the opportunity to view them from any side and to understand how the lines of authority flow. Figure 4 is an example of a circular organizational plan proposed to a body contemplating reorganization.[18]

PREPARING ORGANIZATIONAL CHARTS

Organizational charts sometimes can be misleading as well as contain inaccuracies. Too many details, emphasis on design attraction rather than content accuracy, and lack of clarity are but a few of the problems which can be encountered in early pattern construction. Sayles and Strauss have declared that "organizations should be constructed from the *bottom up,* rather than *top down.*"[19]

Principles to Follow

In developing an organizational structure, most corporate executives look for rules to follow or formulas in which the basic elements of organizational patterning can be substituted. Petersen, Plowman, and Trickett have suggested four steps that must be taken before the conventional organizational chart is designed. These steps include identification of specific objectives of the company, determination of work to be done to accomplish the objectives, separation of work activities into cohesive and functional groups, and a charting of the groupings.[20] For the most part, the following general steps can be used in the design of organizational charts:

1. *Identify goals and objectives of organization.* The establishment of any agency is justified through its aims and objectives. What it is designed to do and what it does (and how successfully) are, in part, attributable to the method by which it reaches its goals. Subgoals and purposes are usually delineated in order that activities be clearly defined and groupings be determined.

2. *Group the goals and objectives of the organization into functional units.* The criterion for grouping and forming units is association. Grouping is brought about by coordinating the interrelated parts of the organization into a harmonious whole. Petersen, Plowman, and Trickett said, "It is the lubricant which overcomes and prevents friction in the highly sensitive human mechanism. It is also the cement which binds the elements of an enterprise together, transforming a collection of differentiated parts and people into an integrated whole."[21]

3. *Form the identified functional groups into depart-*

mental units. For the most part, the arrangement of departmental units evolves from experience and as a result of empirical judgment. What works for one enterprise may not always be the pattern for another. Quite often, clear and discernable relationships come forward and provide the starting point at which the administrator may begin to form units.

4. *Sketch a basic model of the organization and give it a trial run.* Much like the scientist who develops a fundamental principle or law, the executive architect designs what he believes the model will look like. Once the basic sketch has been completed, it is ready for critiquing by line and staff leaders and by those for whom the table of organization will have great significance—the worker. More than any other step in the process of designing an organizational chart, this phase determines its success. For without the necessary involvement of the people for whom the organizational chart will have meaning, the design will have limited acceptance.

5. *Revise the original model according to the input received.* At this point, the executive is ready to put the final product to press. As he nears completion of the design, he should be aware to include, in addition to all other pertinent information, the following:
   a. A descriptive title of the model
   b. A date of final drafting
   c. Some identification of who prepared the chart

6. *Evaluate the final design by assigning to each of the functional groups and levels the names of all individuals who work within the organization.* This, the final step, becomes a measuring stick by which the model is judged for accuracy and completeness. If each individual is to realize his involvement with and his place in the organization, then each must be able to be located within the design model.

USES OF ORGANIZATIONAL CHARTS

For the executive, the table of organization becomes a picture of the enterprise in schematic form. For the people in a unit or division it clarifies the work in which their activity ultimately takes place. Therefore, chart use finds its applications in many ways. Petersen, Plowman, and Trickett suggest some of the following methods of chart utilization: promotion, communication, analysis, and portrayal.[22] In addition to these, some of the following uses can be made of charts:

1. *Orientation.* As a method for indoctrinating the new person coming into an organization or the promoted individual moving to a new position, the chart is very effective.
2. *Recruitment.* One of the frequent questions asked by new management prospects is, "What does your table of organization look like?" The chart of the organization becomes a most valuable tool in the recruitment of new personnel into an organization. It helps the prospective member better understand what his role is and helps clarify his relationship to other members.
3. *Public relations.* Any large organization has its share of visitors. Important to any such visit is information that can be simplified and shared. The organizational chart usually is one of the best pieces of information since its use is generally well understood, and its simplicity makes it easy for an organizational spokesman to display during tours and at speaking engagements. In addition, any informational pamphlets usually include such charts.
4. *Evaluation.* One of the unique ways that an organizational chart can be used is as a follow-up measure to personnel selection and as a periodic review and update. Quite often, after an organization has been operating for a period of time under an established pattern, the corporate manager can use the latest organizational table as a vehicle for evaluation. He may ask the personnel:
   a. Does the table show clearly your level of responsibility in the organization?
   b. Is your relationship to those around you shown in the table of organization?
   c. What changes would you make in the present organizational table to better clarify your role and better identify what the organizational pattern really is?

IMPLICATIONS FOR THE FIELDS OF PHYSICAL EDUCATION, RECREATION, AND ATHLETICS

For many years, texts concerned with the administration of physical education took the traditional approach by reporting on many of the aspects of administration from a practical point of view. These writings focused on aspects of the programs that reflected the parochial concerns of administrators. Minimal attention was given to the behavioral aspects of administration and a little more to the contemporary writings of authors in other fields, particularly those in political science and business administration. One of the first to break away from the traditional approach by reporting on the processes of administration in physical education and athletics was Zeigler. He proclaimed that it is necessary for administrative members of physical education and athletics to align themselves with the more progressive trends in education.[23]

Recreation, a profession that has as its basic foundation for course work the social sciences, has contemporized its literature in administration by utilizing much of the material written by authors mentioned earlier in this chapter. Rodney was quick to include in his text written on administration in recreation, some of the more modern research as a "new" approach to administration.[24] Esslinger, in his recently revised edition of a book on administration, completely modified the approach to laying a foundation for administration theory in physical education by focusing on the human behavior aspects.[25]

If there is a lesson to be learned, it would be that administrative theory in physical education and athletics must be based on field research in all areas of administration. No longer can the physical education dean and the intercollegiate athletic director be content with including in their libraries only books written by prominent professionals in the field of physical education. Ordway Tead focused his attention on the what, why, and how of administrative work in top management.[26] Vance Packard in writing *The Pyramid Climbers*[27] and William Whyte in his book *The Organization Man*[28] focused their remarks on the attributes of the successful executive. These and many other authorities have a rich background in market research and administrative theory with which anyone contemplating an administrative career must be conversant.

For the public school physical education administrator, greater attention must be placed on the internal function of the supervisory and directory position within the educational framework than on the duties and responsibilities described by normative surveys. The effectiveness of the leader's position in enriching the learner's potential should be the major focus, rather than the efficiency of the organizational pattern.

For the recreational administrator, the more modern approach is to broaden the program of preparation to include a larger range of experiences and competencies. Quite often, the recreational executive finds that his duties entail many responsibilities similar in scope to the junior executive of the business enterprise. More

recent developments in recreational administrative training include the growth of in-service management seminars in executive
development. Efforts in these short courses have been to enrich
the skills of the manager in decision making, problem analysis,
forecasting and planning, supervision, budgeting, evaluation, and
public relations, to include a few.

In junior college, senior college, and university physical education and athletic administration, the training of the administrator
is much different. The tripartite function of the professional leader—teaching, research, and extension service—creates a different
kind of organizational pattern giving it autonomy, homogeneity
and heterogeneity as well as singleness of purpose. Wilson put
it rather succinctly when he said, "The prevailing attitudes toward
college administration are at about the same level as were those
toward administration of public school districts a half-century ago,
that is, the administrator should be chosen from the faculty ranks
upon his qualifications of scholarship or seniority."[29] The organizational and administrative patterns for two-year junior college programs is similar to that found in the "small and limited enrollment"
four-year public and private colleges—that is, quite simple.[30]
While larger colleges and universities have formal programs for
executive training, there seems to be a paucity of similar programs for budding executives in physical education and athletics.
As compared to the public school administrator, much of the decision-making function in colleges and universities is shared among
the numerous faculties, committees, and substructures of the institution—thus the need for a much more sophisticated organizational pattern.

The patterning of organizations in today's society demands a
greater understanding of the role that individuals have in contributing to the goals and aspirations of a corporate body as well
as the effect that a model has on freeing the individual to do
his job. Departmentation, communication, span of control, and
hierarchical designing are but a few of the considerations that
one must undertake in shaping an organizational model that will
result in goal realization.

In the following chapter, "The Administrative Challenge," Dr.
Cooper discusses in detail the challenges that confront the individual who aspires to become an administrator.

NOTES

[1] Robert E. Wilson, *Educational Administration* (Columbus, Ohio:
Charles E. Merrill Books, 1966), pp. 341–3.

[2] Alan C. Filley and Robert J. House, *Managerial Process and Organizational Behavior* (Glenview, Ill.: Scott, Foresman and Company, 1969), p. 69.

[3] Richard A. Johnson, Fremont E. Kast, and James E. Rosenzweig, *The Theory and Management of Systems,* 2d ed. (New York: McGraw-Hill Book Company, 1963), p. 58.

[4] Johnson, Kast, and Rosenzweig, *Theory and Management,* pp. 58–63.

[5] Edgar L. Morphet, Roe M. Johns, and Theodore L. Reller, *Educational Organization and Administration: Concepts, Practices, and Issues,* 2d ed. (Englewood Cliffs, N.J.: Prentice-Hall, 1967), pp. 98–110.

[6] Johnson, Kast, and Rosenzweig, *Theory and Management,* pp. 63–5.

[7] Wilson, *Educational Administration,* p. 60.

[8] Morphet, Johns, and Reller, *Educational Organization,* p. 92.

[9] Elmore Petersen, Grosvenor E. Plowman, and Joseph M. Trickett, *Business Organization and Management,* 5th ed. (Homewood, Ill.: Richard D. Irwin, 1962), p. 149.

[10] Petersen, Plowman, and Trickett, *Business Organization,* pp. 156–7.

[11] Ibid., pp. 167–78.

[12] David R. Hampton, Charles E. Summer, and Ross A. Webber, *Organizational Behavior and the Practice of Management* (Glenview, Ill.: Scott, Foresman and Company, 1968), p. 189–94.

[13] Leonard R. Sayles and George Strauss, *Human Behavior in Organizations* (Englewood Cliffs, N.J.: Prentice-Hall, 1966), p. 321.

[14] Sayles and Strauss, *Behavior in Organizations,* p. 332.

[15] Hilda C. Kozman, ed., *Developing Democratic Human Relations through Health Education, Physical Education, and Recreation* (Washington, D.C.: American Association for Health, Physical Education, and Recreation, 1951), p. 401.

[16] Hampton, Summer, and Webber, *Organizational Behavior,* p. 275.

[17] Petersen, Plowman, and Trickett, *Business Organization,* p. 223.

[18] American Association for Health, Physical Education, and Recreation, "Committee to Develop a Preliminary Design for Converting AAHPER into a Federation," *JOHPER,* (June, 1968), p. 62.

[19] Sayles and Strauss, *Behavior in Organizations,* p. 467.

[20] Petersen, Plowman, and Trickett, *Business Organization,* p. 54.

[21] Ibid., p. 180.

[22] Ibid., pp. 236–9.

[23] Earle F. Zeigler, *Administration of Physical Education and Athletics* (Englewood Cliffs, N.J.: Prentice-Hall, 1959), p. 11.

[24] Lynn S. Rodney, *Administration of Public Recreation* (New York: Ronald Press Company, 1964), pp. 26–54.

[25] Edward F. Voltmer and Arthur A. Esslinger, *The Organization and Administration of Physical Education,* 4th ed. (New York: Appleton-Century-Crofts, 1967), pp. 1–5.

[26] Ordway Tead, *The Art of Administration* (New York: McGraw-Hill Book Company, 1951), pp. 1–6.

[27] Vance Packard, *The Pyramid Climbers* (New York: McGraw-Hill Book Company, 1962), pp. 143–57.

[28] William H. Whyte, *The Organization Man* (New York: Simon and Schuster, 1956), pp. 143–65.

[29] Wilson, *Educational Administration,* p. 329.

[30] Greyson Daughtrey and John B. Woods, *Physical Education Programs: Organization and Administration* (Philadelphia: W.B. Saunders Company, 1971), p. 468.

chapter 3　　The Administrative Challenge

JOHN M. COOPER

A human being who has no scars has not tangled with life.
Anonymous

Often the question is asked, "Why does anyone want to be an administrator?" Certainly there is more stress in being an administrator than there is in being a teaching professor, a typist, or a bookkeeper. The desire for an administrative position is often difficult to explain in light of the experiences to be faced—experiences that range from the trivial to the dramatic. Emotions are often strained. Unsolved problems are carried home where they interfere with sleep. Consequently, the major concern of an aspiring administrator must be his potential for administrative intelligence, stamina, patience, and the pure "guts" to meet the challenge involved in being under daily stress.

Before accepting an administrative assignment, the candidate should do a bit of self-analysis (perhaps also seeking the comments of those whose judgment he respects) concerning his suitability as an administrator. Furthermore, professional psychological and educational advice could be sought, including testing that might indicate aptitudes and appropriate interests. Finally, medical examinations to determine his physical capability to withstand stress should be considered.

The administrative challenge is multidimensional. Certain aspects of this challenge will be discussed here; several others are mentioned elsewhere in this book.

ADMINISTRATIVE CHALLENGES

Being Democratic

Someone has said that democracy is the daughter of discussion. Yet, when matters are consistently handled in a truly democratic fashion, accountability is lost and action is so slow that chaos results. An administrator who is democratic in most situations, can, on occasion, be relatively autocratic and get by with it without difficulty. On the other hand, one who is autocratic in most cases may not appease by being democratic on occasion. There is a time for being democratic and a time for being autocratic, each of which can be effective if the place and time are carefully chosen and each is delicately instituted. A careful blending of democratic and autocratic methods is appropriate for most leaders and acceptable to most followers. Obviously, autocratic procedures usually get the fastest results and are necessary under certain conditions. For example, matters of little consequence are best taken care of by one person.

Voting on membership of committees as well as on large issues is in keeping with effective democratic administration, provided an open-door policy is adhered to administratively. Usually the democratic process is more effective when a policy-making group prepares a set of directives to be followed by the administrator and members in their deliberations.

The administrator may attempt to alleviate stress by being a good fellow, but no matter how democratic he wishes to be, certain responsibilities are his. Barnard discusses two concepts: "the process of coordinated effort" and "democratic decision making."[1] The latter connotes decision by group action yet does not preclude the administrator's gently leading the group while getting serious input from every member. The "process of coordinated effort" means that a decision has been reached and coordinated effort is necessary for the adopted plan to be effective. These two ideas are not necessarily mutually exclusive. In fact, they appear to be definitely related to each other and may under certain conditions be considered as one process.

The process of decision making is a complicated one. Tead has said, "The increasing stress is upon clear responsibility for decisions placed upon legislative bodies for policy determination and upon the actions of a few elective executives for policy execution."[2] The trend is to leave the items that are purely administrative to the administrator and to have a policy-making group develop guidelines for the administrator to follow in his decision making.

Selecting Personnel

This procedure should be a cooperative affair between the administrator and his staff, a concept often difficult for an administrator to realize.[3] Those with whom the selected individual will work should have an opportunity to openly express their opinions. For example, sometimes the salary rate at which the individual would be hired is not in harmony with the present staff salaries. This problem has two possible solutions. One, the most competent, experienced person is offered the position at this higher salary. Present staff members are notified in an informal way of the reason for the salary differential. It must be remembered that in a collective sense an organization is only as effective as its individual members. The hiring of top-notch people helps preserve the competence and integrity of the organization. However, an out-of-line salary rate for a new person can be a source of friction for years.

Two, a younger, less experienced, and unknown individual is selected as a replacement or expansion person at a lower salary than the staff presently receives. This solution is always a gamble, for the choice often does not enhance (at least for a while) the reputation of the organization as a whole. The final decision on such matters is an administrative one.

Hiring procedures used by the administrator or personnel director must be clearly understood so that discrimination of any kind is prevented. Salary differentials must not be made on the basis of race, religion, or sex.

Dealing with Factions

Sometimes an administrator is placed in a position of attempting to soothe the feelings of two or more groups who have real or imagined differences.[4] One such situation occurs when a faculty has a younger and an older group disagreeing on many items. Or it may be that two individuals with power aspirations gather about them certain followers. This situation is usually less well defined, but the lines of demarcation eventually do become apparent when decisions are to be made on particular issues. Differences may be due to sexual, racial, or geographic origin. What does an administrator do in such situations in order to have an effective functioning organization?[5]

Some administrators are able to turn away a factional dispute with the utterance of an unpremeditated soft word or with an unplanned joke. To some members of the group the situation may not be a joking matter and may not be so easily brushed aside.

Perhaps the best way is to carefully plan to avoid having such a conflict occur or at least to prevent its developing to crisis proportions at an inappropriate time.

Some leaders seem to have a quality that might be called administrative intelligence or insight. They seem to use just the right words or phrases to quiet tempers. Others go about handling such disputes by making honest attempts to side with neither group. Support is given first to one group and then to the other, depending upon the evident logic of the position and not by whom it was submitted for consideration. As soon as it is clear that judgment will be based on the soundness of the ideas and not on personalities, then the administrator is on firm ground and should (even if grudgingly) receive support for his position. Also, as soon as it is clear to the administrator that selfish and immediate, rather than long-range, goals are the quest of a few, he has a basis for withholding approval of a plan that may not be well founded.

Sometimes, such groups are never entirely subdued until they are outnumbered by replacement through retirement, or by the impact of a new administrator who gets the upper hand immediately before he is classified as being a part of any group. A new personality arriving on the scene may change the entire atmosphere.

Ensuring Academic Freedom

Creativity seems to be rooted in the freedom to express oneself without imposition of restrictions. An administrator often is then confronted with how to interpret freedom in all situations and under all conditions. He may have the group impose some limitations on the actions of individuals where their activities may offend others. Upon what grounds does he make a judgment?

When harm is done to people or distortion of the truth is evident, some action is needed. Unless a decision is made at a higher level, a committee of peers usually can serve as a jury and make recommendations upon which the administrator can base his ultimate decision.

The administrator's superiors may have developed policies and guidelines, and it becomes his responsibility to interpret and enforce them. The courts have made rulings concerning procedural boundaries in some matters, a factor that must be borne in mind.

Regardless, the administrator may be forced to take a stand or at least become acutely aware of the activities of some individuals that appear to hinder group action. If the administrator takes action or establishes rules of operation, he will need to have the support of his staff and of his superiors in order to present a united front if challenged by individual members of the group.

Treating Confidential Information

Under given conditions the wisest of administrators may be not as discreet as he should be. There is a fine line between being discreet and indiscreet. Tead asks:

> Are there not in public affairs, for example, in diplomatic dealings, and in private business in crucial policy decisions, issues of a confidential nature requiring inside information which it would be indiscreet if not harmful to have "democratically shared" in some representative group?[6]

Undoubtedly, most administrators have information that is kept in confidence. Some administrators seem obsessed with the need to be secretive about certain matters. To overdo the element of secrecy because of his position is an administrative error. Yet, to release information received in confidence without notifying the proper persons is also a grave mistake. At least, information about recommendations and the persons involved (if personnel are under consideration) should not be divulged until an official announcement is made. In fact, some aspects of the discussions held in the committee meetings may never be made public.

Redirecting Those with Limited Interests

An employee may become so devoted to his job, or to his institution, that he ceases to have outside interests. For all intents and purposes, such persons become married to their positions, often to the neglect of living well-rounded lives. Since respect for employee privacy is paramount in good management situations, what does an administrator do under such circumstances?

This problem, as it has been presented here, is a company or professional matter. To enhance working relationships, the administrator should attempt to redirect such individuals into activities that cause them to spend time in nonprofessional pursuits. Other members of the organization may be casually solicited to help in this endeavor. A building, a school, or a gymnasium should not be thought of as a private possession by the overly devoted employee.

The reverse may be true when an employer expects everyone to be at his beck and call and demands that every employee, from a top executive to a clerk, be an "organization man." A frequently called Sunday afternoon conference is an example of the abuse to which this concept may lead. Staff members should be granted the privilege of private use of their after working hours. It is a challenge to the top executive to refrain from encroaching on the private lives of employees, particularly his immediate subordinates.

Reacting Appropriately

Each situation and each person is so different that an alert administrator considers every possible factor before ever passing judgment.[7] A technique used successfully in a given environment may be unsuccessful in another. A given set of conditions is seldom duplicated at a subsequent date: the time of day, the bodily reactions of each person involved, the temperatures inside and outside, the immediately previous experiences, and the attitudes of those present during the assessment period all influence the ultimate outcome.[8] It could be stated that the administrator is comparable to a computer in that he must be programmed often to be able to react suitably to each new condition.

The appropriate type of administrative reaction demands creative judgment—the ability to produce in a constructive way a totally new environment for each situation, an environment that is conducive to favorable and harmonious settlement of each problem. In a sense the participants are members of an orchestra and the administrator is the conductor blending all instruments into melodious sound.

Fitting People into Appropriate Assignments

Many basketball coaches believe that a competent coach is able to select only four of the five starters on his team without any difficulty. It is thought that at least ten top coaches would agree with his selection of four of these players. One starter may, in their opinion, not be the one to select for a starting berth. Thus, one basketball player on each team may not be the most competent for that position. The percentage of those misassigned is considered to be even greater in education, business, and industry. Many people are selected for positions for which they are unsuited by temperament and even by training.[9] Consequently, these people are unhappy and often become potential troublemekers. The administrator is neither omnipotent nor clairvoyant. In making assignments, it would be most appropriate for him to consult his immediate subordinates, after he has carefully studied the records of the person under consideration. Many institutions use a screening committee for the purpose of formulating personnel recommendations. However, the final decision must rest with the administrator.

Knowing Strengths and Weaknesses

One of the most difficult tasks an administrator faces is to know his own strengths and weaknesses and to be able to evaluate himself objectively in terms of effective decision making. For example, he may believe he has commendable traits such as initiative, good judgment, integrity, courage, stability, fairness, and dependability. However, because the meanings of such terms are highly subjective, the outstanding characteristics an administrator thinks he has and his qualifications as seen by persons who work with him, can be quite different.

Under certain circumstances, one key trait used to the maximum may offset several poor ones. An administrator who is very fair-minded may so impress his colleagues that they support him almost without question. He gets the job done in spite of some handicaps. This may be analogous to the good baseball hitter who exhibits poor batting mechanics except the key one of keeping his head stationary throughout most of the swing, thus keeping his eyes on the pitched ball longer than do his teammates.

An administrator who is able to know what others think of him, without soliciting the information, is most fortunate. He is in a position to use his strengths and weaknesses to an advantage in decision making. However, it must be borne in mind that an executive may possess many fine traits and be an extremely competent person; yet the way in which these traits blend together in forming the leader may make him acceptable or unacceptable to those with whom he works.

Exhibiting Good Judgment

Good judgment is a rich mixture of many qualities: foresight, discrimination, decisiveness, and a large amount of practical experience.[10] An administrator should know his people well enough to anticipate some of their actions and to make use of their qualities in a common-sense approach. While decisions should not be made too hastily, procrastination should not prevail. In some cases, things may need to be nipped in the bud while in others, a quiet pocket veto is all that should be required. To always react immediately and decisively to a situation can be disastrous.

Good judgment involves supporting staff members as much as possible. When their actions cannot be supported, they need to be told why. When possible, they should be told in advance. Not to support a staff member under normal conditions causes him to lose confidence in the administrator.

Coping with Difficult People

The art of getting along with people is the secret to the success of most administrators.[11] With so many techniques and approaches to use in accomplishing this task, it is very difficult to select the proper key to unlock the problem door. Perhaps the first step toward solving difficulties is to know the backgrounds of the individuals well enough to understand their actions, motives, responses, and interests. In other words, what makes them tick as they do.

An administrator once developed a rapport with a difficult person by accidentally finding out that he enjoyed growing flowers, especially peonies. Since the administrator grew them too, a common ground for understanding developed which lasted a lifetime, and the difficult person became a close friend. Often the difficult person is not as easily converted. Possible approaches that could be used in a series of meetings with such a person are:

1. Know when the right time and climate for discussion are present.
2. Sense when a meeting with such a person should be terminated and do so.
3. Let him do most of the talking, at least at first.
4. Attempt to clear up the difficulty by the elimination of small annoyances.
5. Make some small concessions in exchange for large concessions on his part.
6. Admit some mistakes have been made but also point out his mistakes and the many good things he has received from the institution.
7. Be firm but sympathetic, honest, and appreciative of his accomplishments.
8. Refrain from getting into an argument with him. Appeal to him to stop some of his tactics but avoid a condescending attitude.
9. Point out the consequences of his actions if they are prolonged.
10. Inform him, in general, of his colleagues' reactions and finally suggest that he might be happier in a new assignment or a new environment if he cannot adapt to this environment in a satisfactory manner.

Obviously, only a few of these ideas are applicable in a given situation. The administrator must know most of the factors surrounding the circumstances before a judgment can be made to utilize a particular approach.

Being Decisive

Most people prefer to work with an individual who is decisive yet is not offensive.[12] Decisiveness is a trait that involves the act of making up one's mind about a proposal, an issue, or a situation. Actually, it connotes being firm and positive in action. However, it does not imply that an administrator who is decisive has not deliberated at length on the proposition at hand. It does mean that a staff member will receive an answer to a question presented by him. Some administrators straddle the fence on many issues, and staff members receive little help with decisions that they are called upon to make. For example, if at budget planning time an executive is indecisive with the budget planners, confusion will exist. Immediate decisions are needed in such situations.

Administrators who keep candidates for a position dangling for any length of time find themselves selecting mediocre ones because the best ones have accepted positions elsewhere. Good staff members are secured through decisive action in utilizing proper recruitment procedures.

Instituting Change

Change often provokes resistance.[13] An effective administrator recognizes that if change is to be accepted, it must come from within an institution or from an individual. The staff's apparent acceptance of an idea is no proof that, when the chips are down, support will be forthcoming. A change promoted by someone else is, in a sense, a vehicle for harboring hidden resistance that may surface at an opportune moment. The most effective way to bring about change is to have those who might be most affected by it take part in the discussions and have some of their recommendations incorporated for implementation. Persons who believe, with or without justification, that they helped to conceive an idea respond more favorably to the changes it brings.

Imposition of change from the upper echelon of an institutional hierarchy is more likely to be vigorously resisted than if the change is a cooperative venture. Pockets of resistance are often eliminated when resisters are given a voice in the change proceedings. For example, curriculum-construction experts have long recognized that curricular changes are best received and used when the consumers have an active part in the development of the new curriculum.

Recently, the author was invited to a campus where it was stated that the staff had unanimously approved a new direction in curricular design. Since two of the staff had been excluded from the planning meetings but were then asked to vote on the changes, they saw the handwriting on the wall and voted in the affirmative. However, when an outsider arrived and asked for their opinions, they openly expressed opposition, much to the amazement of the planners.

For the best reception, proposed changes in staff assignments and responsibilities should be planned with those involved. Reorganization of a department or a section usually can be done without a resulting crisis if all people involved have a chance to express their opinions. However, the time eventually arrives when a final decision has to be made. Normally, the administrator would be unwise to initiate changes to which most of his staff are opposed, unless directed to do so by his superiors.

Perhaps he may wish to test or air new concepts in the hope that his staff will be receptive to the tentative proposals. In any event, he should document his ideas very carefully. This could include comparison of numbers of students in the various fields, the trends in other institutions, and forthcoming financial support. He may invite outside experts to present their reactions to some of the new concepts. He may then wish to let the ideas germinate before he begins to seriously cultivate them in discussion.

The approach to this problem may be developed through a series of staff meetings designed to select priorities. Hopefully, by this means the staff will choose some proposed changes vital to their welfare, ask that a study be made of them, and that recommendations be proposed for consideration. Although there may be residual opposition, by now the support should outweigh the resistance. Thus, changes can be instituted as gradually or as rapidly as the need dictates.

Creating a Self-motivating Climate

Promises, promises, but very few ever kept, can be said of some administrators. Enlightened personnel experts know that there is more to a job or a position than salary and hours of work. Most individuals want an administrator who helps create an atmosphere in which they are motivated to do their best. This involves making and keeping promises.[14] What climate for action develops the best self-motivated work habits?

To stimulate better employer-employee relations, the administrator:

1. Listens to ideas and concepts not his own.
2. Attempts to refrain from being moody and noncommunicative with his fellow workers.
3. Keeps his subordinates informed on most issues.
4. Creates an atmosphere of job security and chance for advancement.
5. Has moral integrity and avoids a suspicious attitude toward his staff. Utilization of the divide and conquer technique usually results in back biting.

6. Is respected for what he does and stands for regardless of whether the group likes him personally.
7. Avoids an attitude of condescension toward those who work under him.
8. Gives credit verbally, written, and in public where appropriate to those who have done the work. Appreciation is shown for good accomplishment.
9. Is able to conduct business in an informal and casual setting without seeming to do so.
10. Remembers that statistics do not often apply to individuals, but to groups.

It might be said that in a sense the administrator creates the climate for action by his own deeds. Perhaps Heron's[15] comment is appropriate in summarizing this topic: "United aims are not alone the product of goodness but of wisdom."

The comments made in response to the administrative challenge presented in this chapter are to be considered only as guides. Very few human beings are capable of fulfilling in a consistent manner the requirements suggested in this discussion. It is the striving to become effective that makes the effort productive and worthwhile and seasons the administrator.

In the following chapter, "Promoting and Maintaining Human Effectiveness," Dr. Frost discusses the values, principles, and theories of management relating to personnel maintenance.

NOTES

[1] Chester I. Barnard, *Organization and Management* (Cambridge: Harvard University Press, 1948).

[2] Ordway Tead, *The Art of Administration* (New York: McGraw-Hill Book Company, 1951), p. 28.

[3] James K. Van Fleet, *Guide to Managing People* (West Nyack, N.Y.: Parker Publishing Company, 1968).

[4] Ibid.

[5] Bertram M. Gross, *Organizations and Their Managing* (New York: The Free Press, 1964).

[6] Tead, *Art of Administration*, p. 42.

[7] Perrin Stryker, *Character of the Executive Eleven Studies in Managerial Qualities* (New York: Harper and Brothers, 1960).

[8] Tead, *Art of Administration*.

[9] John M. Pfiffner and Frank P. Sherwood, *Administrative Organization* (Englewood Cliffs, N.J.: Prentice-Hall, 1960).

[10] Stryker, *Executive Eleven Studies*.

[11] Mortimer R. Feinberg, *Effective Psychology for Managers* (Englewood Cliffs, N.J.: Prentice-Hall, 1965).

[12] Stryker, *Executive Eleven Studies*.

[13] Warren G. Bemis, Kenneth D. Benne, and Robert Chin, *The Planning of Change* (New York: Holt, Rinehart, and Winston, 1962).

[14] Feinberg, *Effective Psychology.*

[15] Alexander R. Heron, *Beyond Collective Bargaining* (Stanford: Stanford University Press, 1948), p. 213.

BIBLIOGRAPHY

March, James G. and Simon, Herbert A. *Organizations.* New York: John Wiley and Sons, 1966.

chapter 4

Promoting and Maintaining Human Effectiveness

REUBEN B. FROST

*Esprit de corps applies to a unit as a whole. It is a mental state
that represents the sum total of all forces that make for
cohesion, for sticking together, for organized willing endeavor.*[1]
Edward Munson

The success of an organization is measured by the extent to which
its objectives are accomplished, its aims achieved, and its goals
reached. Such objectives, aims, and goals (if their achievement
is to symbolize success) must be worthy ones which ultimately
contribute to the betterment of a society and the greater fulfillment
of its people. These purposes can be realized only when the spirit
of the organization is such that it generates enthusiasm, unselfish-
ness, determination, and dedication.

Esprit de corps denotes high morale, pride in group standards
and group achievements, singleness of purpose among members
of the organization, a willingness to subordinate selfish interests
for the good of the group, and enthusiastic support for the efforts
of its leaders. It includes a high regard for the traditions of the
organization, a spirit of cooperation, fellowship and comradeship,
and an integrity of the group that is able to withstand considerable
buffeting from within and without. Loyalty to one another and
to the enterprise is a mark of esprit de corps and is engendered
only when the goals and purposes are recognized as being deserv-
ing of the strenuous effort and the enthusiastic investment of self.

Many diverse factors contribute to the development of esprit
de corps. These vary somewhat from one situation to another, but
the basic ingredients are quite similar. Good working conditions,
adequate compensation, reasonable security, staff loads that are

not too burdensome, and opportunities for advancement are practical, personal considerations in which all are interested. Facilities that make possible good programs, equipment that is well maintained, and sufficient financial resources to support a sound operation are the concern of most staff members. Because the provision of these factors is the function of good administration, it seems reasonable to conclude that management holds the key to high morale.

THE ROLE OF MOTIVATION

Realization of the full potential of an organization is not simple. Many complex and interrelated variables are involved. The administrator is concerned primarily with the individual and group dynamics that hold the most promise for the attainment of maximum productivity, high quality workmanship, sympathetic and effective guidance, intelligent research, and inspirational teaching. Motivation, as one such significant variable, is discussed here.

Incentives as Motivating Factors

People work to earn a livelihood and to gain a reasonable degree of security. College staff members, like many others, also work hard to be able to take vacations and to fill their leisure with activities that enrich their lives. Some look forward to travel, others to a life of peace and quiet, while many look eagerly toward retirement years which will permit them to do things for which they have never found time.

None of these incentives, however, yields the kind of effort and commitment needed for true excellence, for superlative performance, or for inspired achievement. Motives that merely satisfy the obvious material desires of man without touching the more subtle and deep aspirations seldom call forth the eager and earnest individual effort or arouse the intense and devoted group loyalties needed for creative accomplishments.

Supportive Relationships as Motivating Factors

Rensis Likert discusses the "Principle of Supportive Relationships as an Organizing Concept." He describes this as an "integrating principle" and summarizes research findings that indicate its significance in the building of a capable and effective organization. Likert states this principle as follows:

The leadership and other processes of the organization

must be such as to ensure a maximum probability that in all interactions and all relationships with the organization each member will, in the light of his background, values, and expectations, view the experience as supportive and one which builds and maintains his sense of personal worth and importance.[2]

Ordway Tead, in discussing administration as an art, puts it in these words:

The consensus of study and experience is well-nigh conclusive that where friendly appeals are made by congenial and trusted leaders, where the attractiveness and importance of group goals are made clear, where group pride is built up, where the personal stake of each person in the group outcomes is clearly grasped by all, where the leader has a personal concern and solicitude for the integrity and promise of each member of his group—where this whole body of conditions is being realized, the resulting group behavior will be productive and happy to an optimum degree.[3]

Thus, two men, one a behavioral scientist and one a highly regarded authority on administration, have come to essentially the same conclusion. They repudiate the idea that personal wealth, profit making, and the satisfaction of material wants are the predominant and controlling motives in organizational enterprise. The emphasis is rather on the individual's feeling of personal worth, his perception of himself as an important member of a functioning team, and his awareness that he is gradually realizing his potential.

Staff members, to be most effective, must see the goals and purposes of the institution and the department as worthy of their best efforts; feel that in working toward these goals they are also achieving a high degree of self-realization; and recognize meaningful relationships between their own efforts and achievements and the accomplishment of the purposes of the department and the institution.

It is also important that each individual view his work as challenging and sometimes even difficult. If it does not call for strenuous effort and creative thinking, it becomes monotonous and meaningless. A sense of personal worth and importance is maintained only when all the capabilities, ingenuities, and resources of the individual are called upon. When this occurs, and when the efforts of staff members are perceived as contributing in a significant way to the education of the students and eventually the betterment of society, the relationships will be seen as supportive.

Motivation, a Complex Phenomenon

Frost, in summarizing the chapter "Motivation and Arousal," says:

> Motivation is a complex, important, and often incomprehensible phenomenon. The biological complexities of the human organism, the understanding of social determinants of behavior and the environmental influences of culture, parents, and climate are involved.[4]

Numerous concepts of personality development and motivation support these words. Psychologists, in attempting to explain the phenomena involved in human motivation, employ various terms: instincts, original tendencies, incentives, urges, drives, desires, and needs. Others have formulated theories and principles based on the concepts of libido, homeostasis, self-concept, aspiration, tension, and conflict. In such considerations, analyses of group dynamics must, of course, also be involved.

Rather than attempt to deal with motivation through a review and analysis of its many theories, let us try to simplify the process through a discussion of some of the variables that, for most human beings, influence behavior. Key concepts involved include the following:

1. In a state of perfect equilibrium (homeostasis) there is no urge to act. A certain degree of deviation from this state is necessary before behavior is influenced. When all wants are satisfied, there will probably be no action. The tension built up when equilibrium is disturbed sensitizes the organism and assists in the creation of a state of readiness where the individual is motivated to act. Some arousal is therefore necessary if purposeful action is to occur.

2. For an understanding of motivation, it is necessary to analyze the ways in which behavior is initiated, how it is sustained, the factors that direct and control it, and how it is stopped. Motivation is involved in all of these.

   Newman, Summer, and Warren indicate the significance of the administrator's role and the complexity of motivating the behavior of subordinates when they say:

   > Guiding and motivating the behavior of subordinates has many facets. Plans have to be communicated to subor-

dinates meaningfully, for some explanation of the purposes of, and reasons behind, a particular action usually aids an employee in understanding plans and helps develop his motivation. Inevitably, as plans are being executed, questions of interpretation arise and adjustments are needed to overcome minor difficulties. Enthusiasm for doing a job well needs to be generated. Frictions between workers have to be resolved. Adjustments to allow for Joe's wife being sick or Bob's car breaking down have to be considered. A man's disappointment over a failure to get a desired transfer may open the way for friendly counseling. Men on new assignments have to be trained. Carelessness and infractions of rules call for disciplinary action. Work well done should be recognized. And in all such guiding and motivating, equitable treatment of all subordinates must be reconciled with differences in individual needs.[5]

3. The need for security and survival is a powerful motive in situations where it is not already satisfied. Staff members cannot work effectively if they are worried about how to feed their families or pay the doctor bills. In this segment of our affluent society, however, almost everyone is well enough, safe enough, comfortable enough, and nourished enough, so that the basic needs for food, water, warmth, and security are not the impelling forces that initiate and control behavior. Certainly, few staff members in departments of physical education find these their most compelling motives. Gellerman's words have meaning:

For those people who are not hobbled by dependency, the basic need is not for comfort but a challenge—something tough enough to pit their skill and ingenuity against. To some degree we have an outlet for this kind of hunger in various kinds of research and planning work or in the "creative" hobbies that are so often prescribed as releases from boredom. But most people have to earn their livings in rather routinized ways; and hobbies, for all their variety, have a limited appeal. There remain a vast number of people for whom life in general and their jobs in particular have become just plain dull.[6]

4. Social incentives influence man's behavior more than is generally realized. To be liked and esteemed by one's peers, to be a member of the in-group, to be invited to parties and social functions, to be elected

to offices, to be popular with the students—these and many other evidences of the respect and affection of colleagues and subordinates are factors that frequently influence decisions and actions. Administrators must be conscious of, and understand, this phenomenon as it operates in their own decision-making processes, in their dealings with members of their staff, and in the interactions that continuously take place among employees.

5. Many different urges, drives, and needs act upon and influence a given individual in each specific situation. Sometimes these support each other, and at other times they are in conflict. For example, a faculty member may desire a promotion and therefore strive to placate his immediate superior. At the same time, he may be scheduled for a face-to-face conference in which he feels it will be his obligation to bring a serious point of disagreement to his superior's attention. In another situation, a faculty member may be asked by a department head to state an opinion as to whether or not his friend and colleague should achieve tenure. He believes that the fellow teacher is not capable and productive enough to warrant a strong positive recommendation, and yet his affection for him is so great that he cannot bring himself to offer an objective and honest appraisal. Such conflicts between personal sentiments and objective judgments cause many faculty members to be ambivalent and prevent them from rendering honest judgments. In the above cases, conflicting motives result in difficult decisions and often inconsistent and unpredictable behavior.

6. Loyalties to the various individuals and groups with whom a person works may cause problems in decision making. A person with high ideals of loyalty, who is in a supervisory position, may be caught between his desire to support his staff and his deep feeling of loyalty to his superiors. He must be concerned about the personal welfare of those for whom he feels responsible but cannot, by work or deed, be disloyal to his superiors. He must, in such instances, be sensitive to deeper and more meaningful motives. Influencing his final decision will be: the welfare of the enterprise, his sense of responsibility towards subordinates and superiors, the affection (or lack of it) for the individuals involved, his own per-

sonal ambition, and his heritage of moral and ethical values.

7. Motives pertaining to self-hood are, for many, the strongest influences in their choices of behavior. Each person develops a *concept of self* that includes both the way he perceives himself and the way he believes others perceive him. Self-discovery, self-acceptance, and self-esteem are important in the development of the personality and are related to the expectations that the individual has for himself and those he believes others have for him. They affect the way he perceives his role in a given situation, thereby influencing his behavior. An administrator who has an image of himself as a fair, just, and objective person strives to live up to that ideal. A staff member, knowing that others expect him to be a reasonable, hard-working, reliable individual will probably be that kind of a person in most situations. One who has a self-image of a fighter, and who believes others see him as such, is influenced to act out the role of fearless champion of the staff. The person who has built a reputation as the objective, intelligent, negotiator is inclined to fulfill those expectations. Expectations influence both the behavior of the subordinate and the superior. Snygg and Combs summarize it in these words:

> The meanings which lie in his phenomenal field are the crucial factors in his behavior. It is not the externally observed demand which governs a person's behavior but the phenomenal demand; that is, the role which the individual perceives to be required of him in any situation.[7]

8. The need for challenge and for a feeling of achievement is being increasingly recognized as a powerful determinant of behavior. In interviews with coaches and athletes, it was found that the reaction to challenge and the impelling need for achievement were two of the basic motivating forces which caused athletes and teams to perform unusually well.[8] Peak performances resulted when great athletes with strong competitive urges were challenged to exceed their previous marks, to beat their opponents, to upset favorites. The feeling of accomplishment and the satisfaction of the need to achieve appear to be important motivating factors for those athletes who ultima-

tely win championships. Robert Giegengach, former coach of the United States Olympic Track and Field Team in Tokyo, emphasizes this concept in these words:

> The great champion over the years is the man who wants to win and must win all the time. There is nothing ungentlemanly about this. Some of the mildest people who walk the face of the earth are some of the most vicious when it comes to competition. A complete dissatisfaction with being in a subsidiary position—this must be the motivation of the great champion competitively. Others are satisfied with making the team, being the second man, with being on the squad, with having improved their condition, and similar objectives. The great champion feels a tremendous need to be first.[9]

9. The pride that individuals take in the excellence with which they perform their tasks, the satisfactions that come from the knowledge that their contributions are part of a greater work, and the discovery of a cause to which they can give themselves completely, satisfy deeply felt needs. Self-actualization, self-fulfillment, and self-realization are the profound, ultimate motivating forces for long-term, high-level performance. The realization that the individual is, at least in some measure, fulfilling his destiny provides the ultimate satisfaction that can come from doing one's job, and doing it well. Gellerman, in writing about the related role of management, summarizes this thought as follows:

> It seems to me that the greatest challenge facing management today is to meet this need for a feeling of accomplishment and significance in people's work. Our great need now is for working atmospheres in which latent creativity, deftness, or just plain love of hard work can blossom forth. Boredom is not so much a problem in itself as it is a symptom of management's newest frontier—*maximizing the achievement potential of its people.*[10]

THE ROLE OF THE ADMINISTRATOR

An administrator has many functions. One of the most important is staff leadership. In this capacity he must, if his leadership is to be effective, counsel, encourage, cajole, energize, and inspire his staff. A thorough knowledge of the psychology of motivation and of the many different influences that affect the behavior of individuals is an indispensable adjunct in management.

John Gardner in his treatise on *Excellence* emphasized the importance of high motivation for leaders:

> We must understand that high motivation is as precious a commodity as talent and that if we do not have a system which selects for this attribute as well as for talent, we shall have to resign ourselves to a good deal of flabbiness in our leadership ranks. And we must recognize that one way of bringing highly motivated people to the top is to impose barriers which must be hurdled on the way to the top.[11]

It is essential, therefore, that the administrators themselves be motivated to carry forward the goals of the institution for which they work. It is also necessary, if these goals are to be achieved, that they become the aims and purposes for which all personnel in the organization strive. Only with shared goals can the enterprise move forward toward the realization of the purposes for which the educational institution of which they are a part was founded. In the words of Gardner:

> . . . excellence implies more than competence. It implies a striving for the highest standards in every phase of life. We need individual excellence in all its forms—in every kind of creative endeavor, in political life, in education, in industry— in short, universally.[12]

The Recognition of Individual Differences

Each person, whether he is aware of it or not, sees himself as a distinguishable individual—separate and distinct from other individuals. It is important to him to be treated as an individual and to have a sense of personal worth. Depersonalization and loss of personal identity is associated with alienation, apathy, and sometimes hostility. A leader cannot be effective unless he understands that each staff member reacts differently, that similar leadership techniques cannot be employed with all, and that it is the administrator's responsibility to know each one as a person.

People undergo role changes: they react in some instances as members of a group and in others on an individual basis. They are leaders in some situations and followers in others. It is the responsibility of management to effectively utilize the talents of each staff member in his respective role in varying situations. This can be done if an administrator not only takes pains to become acquainted with each of his subordinates but also utilizes modern scientific techniques in dealing with individual differences.

In their book, *Strategy in Handling People,* Ewing Webb and John Morgan speak in practical terms:

> In dealing with people whom you wish to control or influence, consider all the points of difference that set them apart from others: the traits of their characters, their capacity, their special problems, wants and interests. Plan to treat each person differently in the light of his own nature and viewpoint. Be on the lookout for clues that reveal traits of character and ability. Be on the alert for tell-tale trifles. Try to understand what trait lies back of actions that are unusual, even if they seem trivial. And above all, be sure to make use of every bit of information about people which you already possess.[13]

It is obvious that, while there are commonalities in the cultural influences that shape the personalities of physical education staff members as well as numerous characteristics that are similar, there are also differences which may indicate the most effective approach in each case. A high-strung, emotional person needs to be treated differently from a phlegmatic, rational type; an ambitious coach with a high regard for winning records is more amenable to certain kinds of appeals than a scholarly research worker who is seldom in contact with the public; a warm, outgoing person may be approached by appealing to his emotions while a reserved, cautious staff member may be influenced by the presentation of evidence.

Even the listing of examples causes problems. There can be no advance prescription for any given situation. Each set of circumstances, each combination of personality traits, each case requires a special approach. The answer, then, lies in patience, in study, in good judgment, in empathy, and in consistent attempts at objectivity and impartiality.

The Pursuit of Excellence

Few people would quarrel with "excellence" as a goal. The idea that what is worth doing at all is worth doing well has long been part of our cultural heritage. Most faculty members in educational institutions today have idealistic standards and are meticulous in their class preparation and instruction. They are concerned about their image and their success and want to be respected for their teaching, their scholarship, and their coaching. They feel a need to be liked by students and fellow faculty members, and they derive a good deal of satisfaction from knowing that their work is of high quality.

There are, however, a few staff members in most educational systems who have lost their zest and enthusiasm, do not see their personal goals and the goals of the institution as supportive, or concentrate so intensely on the narrow segment of education for which they are personally responsible that they are unable to share in the enthusiasm for the larger goals of the department and the institution. Therefore, the administrator may need to make special efforts to revive the sense of esprit de corps.

In the pursuit of excellence it is especially important that the administration set worthy goals; for there can also be "excellence" in the pursuit of objectives that are inimical to education and to society. Every staff member must accept the underlying assumption that the goals for which the organization exists and its members strive are worthwhile and sound.

It is the testimony of teachers, coaches, and most participants that the greatest satisfaction comes from achievements that are earned. Long hours of arduous practice, meticulous attention to detail, careful analysis of strengths and weaknesses, serious efforts to improve, and the giving of oneself completely to the task are factors that most generally result in excellence. They are also the factors that bring lasting satisfaction and fulfillment to those involved.

Creative Leadership

Roger Bellows, in his preface to *Creative Leadership,* states:

> Leadership is something more than management. It has a special meaning which includes *creativeness.* A manager—of a home, school, office, factory, labor union, state—may or may not be a creative leader. Creative leadership involves arranging the situation so that mutual goals and understanding meld people into harmonious teams.[14]

Bellows traces older methods of leadership and indicates that changing times need a new approach. He emphasizes the "poverty of authority" and talks about the "participative leadership that failed." He goes on to an analysis of human needs and discusses the relationship of these to motivation and leadership. He applies concepts of tension, conflict, and social behavior to leadership methods and concludes with a discussion of teamwork and leadership qualities. In his final chapter the following statement appears:

> We see a large difference between leadership and supervision. Leadership is planning and arranging the situation so that the group goes forward in a shared direction to the

satisfaction and benefit of all concerned. Supervision is something less than this: it is merely the act of relaying directions from above and seeing that the slaves do the work. It is a difference between the participative style, which is creative leadership, and the autocratic style, which is mere execution, administration, management, or supervision.[15]

LEADERSHIP SUGGESTIONS FOR ADMINISTRATORS

Thus far some elements of human motivation have been analyzed and related to leadership; the importance of human needs and human relationships has been discussed; some characteristics of creative leadership have been identified; and morale and esprit de corps have been emphasized. Theory without application, however, seems somewhat empty. The remainder of this chapter is therefore devoted to identifying guidelines for leadership. The practice of these, it is believed, will assist an administrator in efforts to promote and maintain human effectiveness in the organization.

1. *Personal Commitment.* The leader must be completely committed to the purposes and goals of an organization. Others cannot be expected to follow if the leader is not dedicated to the cause.
2. *Personal Worth and Dignity.* Each member of the unit must be treated in such a way that his feeling of personal worth and dignity as a human being is enhanced. He must be assigned tasks commensurate with his ability and ambition. He must be assured of his value to the organization.
3. *Group Acceptance.* New staff members as well as new administrators, when first appointed, may find some resistance by the in-group. They must accept this at first and not take it as a personal affront. Special efforts must be made initially to prove oneself worthy of acceptance.
4. *Authority and Responsibility.* Authority must be commensurate with responsibility. To assign duties or functions to a person and then withhold the authority necessary to do a good job is a certain road to eventual defeat. No individual, regardless of his ability, can successfully carry out his responsibilities under these circumstances.
5. *Clarity of Channels.* Everyone should know to whom he reports and who reports to him. Confusion about

this principle leads to uncertainty, hesitation, and often hostility.

6. *Opportunity for Advancement.* Each individual should feel that he has an opportunity for advancement, and personal growth and development. If he is expected to remain with the organization, he should have the opportunity to work toward the realization of his potential.

7. *Rational Problem Solving.* There should be, in the department, a feeling that problems, both personal and professional, can be solved by the use of reason. Rational, rather than emotional or political appeals will then more readily be made.

8. *Participation in Policy Formulation.* Individuals who are affected by a policy should have a voice and should participate in the formulation of policy. In large organizations this may need to be through representation.

9. *Fact Control.* Insofar as possible, decisions should be made on the basis of facts. Every effort should be made to obtain all the facts before the time of decision making.

10. *Recognition for Service.* Every opportunity should be utilized to recognize individuals for meritorious service. Public recognition, private communications, promotions in rank, and raises in pay are means by which this can be achieved.

11. *Security.* Reasonable security is important. Good staff members do not rest on their laurels because they feel secure. They work on organizational goals creatively when worry about jobs and pay is diminished.

12. *Shared Goals.* When plans are shared in the making, they are likely to be shared as they are being implemented. Shared goals are the key to a successful organization.

13. *Pride in the Organization.* When excellence is the motto, when goals are being achieved, when worthwhile accomplishments are evident, when group loyalty exists, pride in the organization will emerge, and individual members will be happy to belong and eager to do their part.

14. *Face-to-Face Communications.* Every opportunity should be taken for face-to-face conferences with staff members. Memorandums, telephone calls, and other impersonal communications are cold and

must be supplemented with warm, human, personal contacts.

15. *Staff Meetings.* Both regularly scheduled and on call staff meetings should be held. Every effort should be made to make these as warm and worthwhile as possible. Staff participation is important.

16. *Knowledge of the Leader.* People do not readily follow a leader who is not knowledgeable about his job, about the tasks of the organization, and about people. It is incumbent on the administrator to study, to read, to participate in professional organizations, to write, and to teach if he is to remain in the forefront.

17. *Thoughtful Concern.* The effective leader has a sincere interest in the personal welfare of all subordinates and their immediate families. Good morale is generally the result of thoughtful concern.

18. *Justice and Impartiality.* While personality problems and clashes are bound to exist in any organization, staff members react much more favorably when they sense that leaders are making every effort to be just and impartial—both when rewards are being parceled out and when disciplinary action is being taken.

19. *Vision.* The leader must have vision. He must see a little farther ahead, a little more clearly, than those who follow. Only in this way can he chart the course and expect others to follow.

20. *Courage.* The great leader must have courage, both physical and moral. The difficult decisions, the unpopular ones, will be his alone to make. The right decision may not be acclaimed by his staff, particularly if that particular course of action should fail. Only the courageous person can remain a leader.

21. *Sensitivity.* The creative leader must be sensitive to the thoughts and feelings of those whom he seeks to lead. Not always does this mean the dispensation of inordinate sympathy and the making of decisions according to group consensus, but it does imply careful consideration of their sentiments and concerns. Decisions must then be made in the light of the circumstances of the moment and the goals.

22. *Perseverance.* Successful leaders possess determination and perseverance. All great enterprises are frustrating at times, and there are many who suggest to the leader that the venture be abandoned. The strong leader, however, persists and moves dogged-

ly ahead even when most of his followers become discouraged and ready to quit. It is indeed in moments like this that the test of the truly great leader comes. Many a struggle has been won because of the determination and perseverance of the leader.

23. *Hard Work.* The leader sets the pace and shows the way. Subordinates are not inspired to work long hours if the leader is indolent. Steady, consistent, hard work on the part of all staff members inevitably brings results in terms of a productive organization and the achievement of its goals.

24. *The Leader Must be Himself.* While one can learn from others, no two leaders are exactly alike. Studies of great leaders reveal that they are cast in many different molds. Each person must be himself.

25. *Giving of Himself.* The truly great leader gives of himself as well as of his knowledge, his administrative ability, and his experience. This is soon recognized by those who surround him. It is the essence of good leadership.

HUMAN EFFECTIVENESS

The promotion and maintenance of human effectiveness is, as has been indicated, the real challenge to administrators. The calling forth of all possible *human resources* requires more than mangerial skills; it is the challenge of creative leadership. Where such leadership exists, latent talent will be discovered, the need for self-expression can be satisfied, and individuals will have a sense of not just being but becoming. Teachers and other staff members will be making an honest effort to produce, for they will feel that they are a significant part of a worthwhile enterprise. They will strive to overlook personality conflicts, fears, and personal problems and work toward shared goals. In short, they will give of themselves as they move forward together in the effort to make their institution and their department as productive as possible. Effective leaders are those who maximize human potential.

In Chapter 5, "Effective Public Relations," Dr. Warren discusses the importance of effective public relations in health, physical education, and recreation programs.

NOTES

[1] Edward L. Munson, *Leadership for American Army Leaders* (Washington, D.C.: Infantry Journal, 1944), p. 69.

[2] Rensis Likert, *New Patterns of Management* (New York: McGraw-Hill Book Company, 1961), p. 103.

[3] Ordway Tead, *The Art of Administration* (New York: McGraw-Hill Book Company, 1951), pp. 51–2.

[4] Reuben B. Frost, *Psychological Concepts Applied to Physical Education and Coaching* (Reading, Mass.: Addison-Wesley Publishing Company, 1971), pp. 86–95.

[5] William H. Newman, Charles E. Summer, and Kirby E. Summer, and Kirby E. Warren, *The Process of Management,* 2nd ed. (Englewood Cliffs, N.J.: Prentice-Hall, 1967), p. 575.

[6] Saul W. Gellerman, *The Uses of Psychology in Management* (London: Collier-Macmillan, 1970), p. 254.

[7] Donald Snygg and Donald Combs, *Individual Behavior* (New York: Harper and Brothers Publishers, 1949), p. 97.

[8] Frost, *Psychological Concepts,* p. 86.

[9] Ibid., pp. 86–95.

[10] Gellerman, *Psychology in Management,* pp. 254–55.

[11] John W. Gardner, *Excellence* (New York: Harper and Row, Publishers, 1961), p. 100.

[12] Gardner, *Excellence,* p. 100.

[13] Ewing T. Webb and John B. Morgan, *Strategy in Handling People* (New York: Garden City Publishing Company, 1930), p. 154.

[14] Roger Bellows, *Creative Leadership* (Englewood Cliffs, N.J.: Prentice-Hall, 1959), p. ix.

[15] Bellows, *Creative Leadership,* p. 305.

BIBLIOGRAPHY

Bell, Wendell; Hill, Richard J.; and Wright, Charles R. *Public Leadership.* San Francisco: Chandler Publishing Company, 1961.

Bischoff, David. "Administrator." *Quest.* NAPECW and NCPEAM, University of Massachusetts, Amherst. Monograph VII (December, 1966).

Bucher, Charles A. *Administrative Dimensions of Health and Physical Education Programs, Including Athletics.* St. Louis: The C. V. Mosby Company, 1971.

Collingwood, Thomas R. and Leonard, Willet. "The Effects of Physical Training Upon Self-concept and Body Attitude." *Journal of Clinical Psychology* vol. 27, no. 3 (July, 1971).

Coopersmith, Stanley. *The Antecedents of Self-Esteem.* San Francisco: W. H. Freeman and Company, 1967.

Daughtrey, Greyson and Woods, John B. *Physical Education Programs: Organization and Administration.* Philadelphia: W. B. Saunders Company, 1971.

Frost, Reuben B. "The Director and the Staff." *Administration of Athletics in Colleges and Universities.* edited by Edward S. Steitz. Washington, D.C.: American Association for Health, Physical Education, and Recreation, 1971.

Gordon, Chad and Gergen, Kenneth J., eds. *The Self in Social Interaction.* New York: John Wiley & Sons, 1968.

Griffiths, Daniel E. *Administrative Theory.* New York: Appleton-Century-Crofts, 1959.

Havel, Richard C. and Seymour, Emery W. *Administration of Health, Physical Education, and Recreation.* New York: The Ronald Press Company, 1961.

Hutt, Max L.; Isaacson, Robert L.; and Blum, Milton L. *Psychology: The Science of Interpersonal Behavior.* New York: Harper and Row, 1966.

Jennings, Eugene E. *An Anatomy of Leadership.* New York: Harper and Brothers, 1960.

Jersild, Arthur T. *In Search of Self.* New York: Teachers College, Columbia University, 1952.

Kennedy, John F. *Profiles in Courage.* New York: Pocket Books, 1956.

Knickerbocker, Irving. "Leadership: A Conception and Some Implications." *An Introduction to School Administration.* New York: Macmillan Company, 1966.

McGregor, Douglas. *Leadership and Motivation.* edited by Warren G. Bennis and Edgar H. Schein. Cambridge, Mass.: The M.I.T. Press, 1966.

Nolte, M. Chester. *An Introduction to School Administration.* New York: Macmillan Company, 1966.

Resick, Matthew C.; Seidel, Beverly, L.; and Mason, James G. *Modern Administrative Practices in Physical Education and Athletics.* Reading, Mass.: Addison-Wesley Publishing Company, 1970.

Ullman, Albert D. *Sociocultural Foundations of Personality.* Boston: Houghton Mifflin Company, 1965.

Voltmer, Edward F. and Esslinger, Arthur A. *The Organization and Administration of Physical Education.* 4th ed. New York: Appleton-Century-Crofts, 1967.

chapter 5   Effective Public Relations

NED WARREN

Public relations originated with early man. Communication and persuasion, as simple forms of publicity, have grown into public relations in its present complex function, now a necessity in literally every aspect of modern life. Business, industry, education, religion, government, and other great enterprises of our civilization owe much of their success to their ability to gain support by changing the attitudes and opinions of people. The development of public relations may be traced through the periods of history in changing terminology; influence, publicity, information, propaganda, public opinion, and many other terms have been familiar designates in its evolution.

In America, public relations had its beginning in the colonial period. Its stages of development were usually intensified during periods of crisis and strife; independence, wars, depression, politics, and social conflict serving as catalysts for changes that required public support. During the last few decades, public relations programs gained widespread support for the economy, institutions, and government. No area of American life today is untouched by programs designed to sway public interest toward products, ideas, or concerns.

Public relations grew from a person-to-person effort to highly organized, scientifically planned programs designed to reach millions of people at the cost of millions of dollars. Programs progressed from local to international scope and now influence world products, ideologies, and politics. Today in America thousands of people are engaged vocationally in public relations programs of various designs. A recent development on the American scene has been the growth of large business firms devoted to merchandising public relations programs and consultations. Vastly increased competition for popular approval and dollar support has made it practically impossible for an enterprise to exist successfully today without a well-designed and successful public relations program. When success is dependent upon the ability to influence opinions and attitudes, then programs must take into account the importance of the interests, desires, and needs of the people concerned.

Public relations programs for the future, though based on the rapidly changing times in which we live, must look to the needs of people in the years ahead. Because of the importance of technology, programs expected to alter opinions and win support of future populations must recognize emerging patterns and predict and plan accordingly.

PUBLIC RELATIONS AND PUBLICS DEFINED

Public relations has many definitions. The wording of any given definition is usually influenced by its source and the inclination of its particular application to the public.

Generally speaking, however, public relations may be defined as planned relationships with other individuals or groups designed to influence understanding, attitudes, and opinions. Such efforts are usually designed to influence opinion and attract support toward certain courses of action.

Public relations has been defined as the activities of an industry, union, corporation, profession, government, or other organization in building and maintaining sound and productive relations with special publics. Another interpretation refers to the art or profession of organizing and developing these activities such as university courses in public relations and requirements for various technical skills. Howard Stephenson defines professional public relations as "the art of convincing people that they should adopt a certain attitude or pursue a certain course of action; usually associated with management."[1] George F. Meredith, former president of the American Public Relations Association, defines public relations as "everything involved in achieving a favorable opinion."[2] Philip Lesly defines public relations as all activities and attitudes intended to judge, adjust to, influence, and direct the opinion of any group or groups of persons in the interest of any individual, group, or institution.[3]

The term *public* as used in the public relations field denotes individuals or groups with special interests and other identifiable characteristics.

Philip Lesly defines publics as any group of individuals that a public relations program seeks to influence.[4] A committee of three may be a public, only as may a firm's stockholders, its employees, its customers, its community; and, too, a legislature, the nation, the world. Cutlip and Center state that a public is "a group of individuals tied together by some common bond of interest—and sharing a sense of togetherness."[5] Howard Stephenson defines a public as a group of people with a common interest.[6]

In this country, the total population includes about as many publics as there are interests and concerns among its people. A public, more than just a large group of people, has identifiable characteristics such as the sharing of a common interest or geographic location. For example, a school or college might have a large public while each of its major activities, such as music or athletics, captures the interest of segments of the institution's public or those outside of the major group. Interests further subdivide into publics with even more specialized interests—the band or the football team.

PURPOSE, PRINCIPLES, AND OBJECTIVES

The purpose of public relations is to influence public attitude and to change, if not control, public opinion and support in accordance with planned objectives.

In planning for effective public relations, it is necessary to bear in mind certain guiding principles of program development:

1. The program should be begun within the confines of the organization itself. This implies the support and thorough understanding of the objectives by all members of the organization.
2. The person charged with the development and conduct of the program along with the public relations staff (the size and organization of which should be dependent upon the job to be done) should be thoroughly familiar with the organization's products and services and what the program is expected to achieve.
3. All factual information possible should be accumulated through the use of records, interviews, studies, surveys, and the like for analysis and use in program planning.
4. The program should be planned on the basis of the results of research and put in appropriate written form to be distributed to all involved personnel for study and understanding.
5. The program should be funded in accordance with its needs and the expected results.

6. In carrying out the planned program, all available resources should be utilized. Effort should be made to involve all personnel who could make a contribution and all media that could be effective in meeting the objectives planned.

7. Continuous evaluation of the effectiveness of the program should be made with accomplishments measured periodically against objectives.

Public relations programs and efforts should have clearly stated objectives. Objectives must demonstrate interest in the needs and welfare of the publics as well as program accomplishment.

Such objectives include:

1. Identifying the public concerned.
2. Providing accurate information for public consumption.
3. Developing awareness in the public concerned.
4. Erasing misconceptions and misunderstanding.
5. Improving relationships with the public.
6. Building interest and stimulating curiosity.
7. Bringing about attitude changes in individuals and the public.
8. Gaining and retaining public support.
9. Assuring that support gained is deserved.
10. Measuring the gains in public attitude and support.
11. Evaluating the program in accordance with objectives.
12. Adjusting program efforts on basis of accomplishments.

FACTORS INFLUENCING PUBLIC RELATIONS

Psychology

Communications with individuals and groups for the purpose of influencing change in accordance with program objectives necessitates knowledge and understanding of their patterns of behavior.

Aspirations

Changing the attitudes of individuals and groups often depends upon raising their aspirations. This is particularly true in seeking public support for education or for public agencies. Aspirations may be raised by contrasting what the public has as opposed to what it could have if it were willing to make the effort. Such contrasts are shown through speeches, films, pictures, posters, panel discussions, and visits to other communities to observe facilities, programs, and leadership. This technique has often been used to gain support for new buildings or for educational programs as well as for other community projects.

Building Knowledge and Understanding

Public opinion and interest are usually dependent upon the level of knowledge and understanding of individuals and publics. Changes of attitude may be brought about by selecting the right time to provide key information which the public needs and wishes to know. This information, if accompanied by reasons for support, often revives or stimulates interest and a desire to know more. Public relations programs should be designed to (1) provide all information possible to the target publics, (2) provide reasons why individuals or groups should render support, and (3) provide information on results which such support will bring. Public relations leaders should follow through by keeping public information updated. New information pertinent to ongoing projects should be provided to keep public opinion and attitude supportive and increasing on a long-range basis.

Motivation

Motivation is difficult to define. The existence of motivation, or lack of it, is a condition of great concern in public relations' attempt to deal with behavior. People act and think in accordance with their motives; therefore, it is imperative that motives be identified and understood. Motives may involve the desire to do good or the desire for material gain. The public relationist must appeal to individual and group motives and often must provide challenging motives to bring about desired behavioral changes.* Motivation research provides knowledge important to the understanding and modification of human behavior.

The above are examples of only a few of the factors that influence success or failure of public relations programs. There are many others including administrative interest, public interest, beliefs and prejudices, levels of education, nature of public response, financial ability of publics, public curiosity and concern, research findings, abilities of personnel, quality of programs or services, staff organization, planning, and evaluation. Public relationists may be confronted with factors such as these in each program. The positive or negative status of each will determine the difficulty of the situation as well as the measure of success or failure. It

---

* The term *relationist* as used with public, community, or human in this chapter refers to the person or persons promoting or having responsibility for promoting public, community, or human relations programs.

is important for the public relations staff to utilize the most favorable of these factors in program planning and include in the planning procedures ways of changing or dealing with the negative factors.

PLANNING AND ORGANIZING THE PUBLIC RELATIONS PROGRAM

There are important steps in planning which give direction to efforts and must be followed if success is to be achieved. Good planning usually precedes success in any endeavor, and public relations is no exception.

A step-by-step procedure for planning has been discussed previously in this chapter under purposes, principles, and objectives and will not be further discussed here; however, Cutlip and Center[7] have presented the following check list to serve as a yardstick to measure planning effectiveness before public relations plans are actually put into effect. Well-planned programs should be:

1. Sincere in purpose and execution.
2. Durable and in keeping with organization's purpose and character.
3. Firm, positive in approach and appeals.
4. Comprehensive in scope and continuous in application.
5. Clear and symbolic, with simple messages.
6. Beneficial to both the sender and receiver of the message.

A sound philosophical approach making use of proper principles of planning and interval checks is important and has educative implications for all who are included in the public relations effort. It is a mistake to allow planning and procedures to get too far ahead of the understanding of those who are considered a part of the public relations team.

It is important to take a long-range view toward developing good public relations. Most enterprises expect to exist over a long period of time and should promote sound procedures in understanding the public and promoting public understanding. There are, however, two approaches to planning in terms of time projections.

Nugent Wedding, professor of marketing at the University of Illinois, has provided definitions of two kinds of programs:[8]

Preventive public relations denotes a long-run program with well-defined and established objects, developed after a thorough study of prevailing conditions. In addition to fulfilling corporate social responsibilities, the underlying purpose of such programs is to maintain continuous cordial relationship with the public by precluding any sources of misunderstanding or friction.

The other type of program, referred to as *remedial,* is of an emergency nature in contrast to the preventive. It is the kind that swings into action when little has been done to forestall some specific crisis that arises.

The above definitions are presented here in contrast to point out that the emphasis should be on the positive, aggressive approach to planning in an effort to ensure long-range programs and results rather than face crisis situations, a common practice.

Organizing for public relations, as in most things, begins with the top person in administration. He must put things in motion as he may well be charged with the success or failure of his creations. Dependent upon the size of the program, he may or may not directly supervise any part of the effort. However, he is responsible for making possible the whole program. Since whatever is done will probably reflect his philosophy of administration, he must have a strong desire to improve public opinion toward the organization he represents and plan accordingly.

The size of the staff organization for public relations is determined by the job to be done. Generally, as the first step, the administrator picks a person to head the public relations effort. The public relations staff may range in size from one individual to scores of staff members. One thing is sure, the staff alone, regardless of size, cannot be the whole public relations team. Each member of the organization has a function to perform and must be sold on the effort. The uncooperative attitudes and actions of a few may destroy the efforts of many.

The cost of a program depends upon the size of the staff and the undertaking. Large staffs which include researchers and expensive research efforts are understandably expensive. Smaller efforts may cost only for released time and the expenses of the printing and distribution of publications. Costs always vary with program objectives.

Interdepartmental cooperation within an organization, business, or institution is very important. It is understandable that strong loyalties develop, and interdepartmental competition is common. This competition is usually good and often stimulates output of goods and services. Loyalty to one's department is also commendable; however, neither situation should put the department ahead of the welfare of the organization or institution as a whole. Public relations programs should be developed so as to inspire employees to cooperate interdepartmentally and develop a team effort in the best interest of the group as a whole. This should be the practice even though the immediate public relations program may not directly involve a certain department in a major way.

Public relations programs cannot answer all problems. All programs have limitations, and this should be well understood at the outset. The existence of a staff and program and the desire to change the attitudes and opinions of individuals or publics does not necessarily bring success. To be successful, a program must be planned and executed with soundness and diligence regardless of the scope of the job to be done.

A very important consideration for success in short- or long-range programs is that good public relations must be deserved. An empty shell is usually discovered all too soon and such discovery may have devastating effects. It is appropriately said of public relations, "You must practice what you preach."

COMMUNICATION IN PUBLIC RELATIONS

The Communication Process

Communication has been variously defined. One definition states that it is a transmission of information, signals, or messages using many media. It is important that the researcher form a personal concept of what communication means.

Communication is the process that allows individuals and groups in any society to share and interchange ideas, attitudes, and/or information, thereby achieving commonality. The advanced communication process has placed man at the top of the animal ladder in intelligence, achievement, and lifestyle.

There are at least two types of communication. There is, first, *singular* communication. In singular communication, as the name implies, the message comes from one source and is transmitted to one or more receivers. Everyone has had experience with singular communication. For example, the politician who speaks may utilize a number of different methods to reach his listeners. He may choose radio, television, or any of a host of other media to speak to the public. But no matter which method he decides upon, his listeners are only receivers of his message. They send no message back to him at the time. It would be quite impossible for the president of the United States, a state senator, or even the city mayor to carry on individual conversations with the many citizens who comprise his public (see Diagram 1).

There is another type of communication that has proved to be more effective than singular communication. This type is known as *cycle* communication. It is characterized by an exchange of ideas, information, or views. People take part in cycle communication daily by exchanging words, facial expressions, and ges-

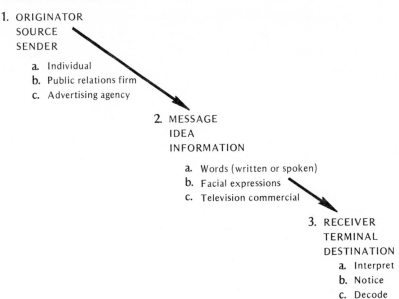

1. ORIGINATOR
   SOURCE
   SENDER

   a. Individual
   b. Public relations firm
   c. Advertising agency

2. MESSAGE
   IDEA
   INFORMATION

   a. Words (written or spoken)
   b. Facial expressions
   c. Television commercial

3. RECEIVER
   TERMINAL
   DESTINATION
   a. Interpret
   b. Notice
   c. Decode

Diagram 1 SINGULAR COMMUNICATION

tures with others, thereby establishing and maintaining understandings and working relationships. Only complete isolation can
prevent cycle communication from taking place (see Diagram 2).

The public relations program should strive to make use of the
most effective type of communication for its specialized purpose.
The situation and circumstances determine which type of communication is most feasible and most desirable.

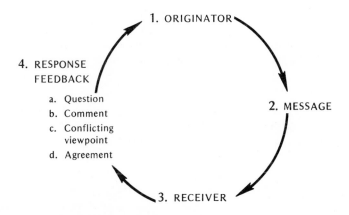

1. ORIGINATOR

4. RESPONSE
   FEEDBACK

   a. Question
   b. Comment
   c. Conflicting
      viewpoint
   d. Agreement

2. MESSAGE

3. RECEIVER

Diagram 2 CYCLE COMMUNICATION

Successful Communication Strategy

There are certain basic factors necessary for any form of communication to be successful. These factors do not guarantee effective communication but must be present if there is any hope for success.

The first factor required for the communication process is an originator (referred to as the sender) to initiate the communication process. The originator may be an individual or an organization with something to communicate to a public.

Another factor necessary for successful communication is the idea, information, or viewpoint (referred to collectively as the message) to be transmitted. The message itself may take many forms; it may appear as written or spoken words, facial expressions, or deliberate actions.

The third factor that must be present for communication to take place is the receiver, that is, the message terminal or destination. An individual, group, or organization may become a receiver to notice, accept, or reject the transmitted message. The action taken by the receiver determines whether or not singular or cycle communication will occur. If the receiver only accepts with no response, singular communication is occurring. Diagram 1 illustrates the process of singular communication.

When the fourth factor, response, comes into play, cycle communication is achieved. Consequently, there is a communication chain established which allows the sender and receiver to reach a common understanding related to the message. Diagram 2 illustrates the cycle communication process.

As can be readily seen in Diagram 2, the only item that distinguishes cycle communication from singular communication is the opportunity for the receiver to respond or give feedback to the sender. At this point, the cycle can begin to recycle and ultimately develop the desired give and take reactions. These responses are vital in communication since the sender can be assured if and how the message is being received and comprehended.

It is readily seen that it is highly possible for a receiver to receive, decode, interpret, or comprehend a message in a form much different from that intended. This is where the true value of feedback can be assessed because it is the response of the receiver to the message. The action or response of the receiver may take the form of debate, agreement, question, or nonaction. Feedback may immediately indicate that the sender has succeeded in transmitting the desired message. In such case, the receiver has taken notice of the message and shares a common understanding; however, this does not necessarily indicate a common agreement. Likewise, feedback may show the sender that the receiver does not share a common understanding of the message. When such a situation exists, the sender has the option of making some alteration or adjustment in communication. A normal reaction would be to take another of many possible approaches since there obviously exists some obstacle in the communication process.

Effective communication is established only when the sender and receiver share a commonness in relation to the message. They may never interpret the message in exactly the same manner since interpretation and comprehension are in terms of experiences and no two people share the same past experiences. However, the communicator must aspire to reach a common and similar understanding with the receiver since this is the only effective communication.[9]

Obstacles to the Communication Process

As previously stated, three factors must be present for communication to occur: a sender, a message, and a receiver. It would be good indeed if these factors assured successful communication. However, even with the presence of a fourth factor, response, there is no such assurance. Response or feedback can only give an indication of whether or not the mechanics of effective communication have been achieved. If the indication is that communication has not taken place, there may be many causes. Individuals, groups, or organizations trying to communicate should be aware of the following possible pitfalls:

1. The sender may not have a clear, concise understanding of the message to be transmitted.
2. The sender may be utilizing ineffective methods for transmitting the message.
3. The purpose of a message may not be distinct to the receiver.
4. The timing may be poor for transmitting the desired message.
5. The content of a message may conflict with the existing information, opinions, and/or attitudes of the receiver.
6. The receiver may simply interpret the message in a manner not at all like the sender's interpretation.
7. The receiver may fail to express or be unable to correctly express his interpretation.

The Communication Media

When the communication process is understood, it is then important to consider some of the tools of communication, often referred to as the media or mass media. Whatever the medium, there are some general characteristics that must be present if communication is to be successful. These characteristics are described by the terms that follow.

Credible. It has been stated that the public interprets in terms of past experiences which have shaped its ideas, attitudes, and opinions. It is very difficult to change these basic interpretations and even more difficult to change them rapidly. For the public relationist this is a key concept. New or different ideas or programs need to be interpreted within the context of older and more basic ones. Credibility is much more than this, however. A public relations program must be truthful. False claims and false advertising do not build a successful business. False praise fails to improve an educational program or an institution. The public relations program should utilize the media to let the public know the *facts* about the services, products, or programs that are available. Future confidence can best be influenced by utilizing creditable information and messages at all times.

Noticeable. Any message that is to be transmitted must obtain the public's notice. If a message goes unnoticed, as many do, it can have no influence or impact on the public. If no one sees, reads, or listens to the message, it is of little consequence, no matter how important the information.

Acceptable. The public may take notice of a message and still be unable to accept it. The message must not contain unbelievable information for the receiver. The acceptability of a message is often related to credibility.

Comprehensible. A message to the public must be in such a form that the public or receiver is able to understand or comprehend. Complicated and deeply structured messages are hazardous to interpretation. Simplicity and directness should be characteristic of each message released.

Illustratable. Many messages are aided by some type of illustration. Here again, a picture is worth a thousand words. Illustrations may precede, accompany, or follow up a message to help establish a meaningful image in the mind of the receiver.

Positive. Messages should be developed constructively and positively in form. A message that calls for action should suggest a course to be taken. The poorer or weaker parts of any program should not be emphasized, although they should be related and positive emphasis should suggest how such programs can be improved. If the message has stimulated an interest and offered some plan of action for the receiver, the sender can hope for success.

Reinforceable. The sender will want to make every effort to follow up and reinforce the message to the receiver. Even if a receiver has interpreted the message in a way desired by the sender, there is no guarantee of action, and most messages call for some type of action. Follow-up may result in the desired action.

Classification of Media

Printed Materials. *Magazines* are very popular with the American public today. A large percentage of the public reads one or more journals or magazines on a regular basis. For many years there was a trend for the public to read the general kind of magazine that included at least one interesting article for everyone. Recently, the American public has indicated through purchases that they prefer magazines that appeal to specialized interests; consequently, some magazines have had to cease operations. Although this may not necessarily be good, the public relationist, because of it, has an easier job. He may now more readily define his public, determine its main interests, and utilize the magazine(s) most likely to be read by the specific public with which he desires to communicate.

Newspapers make their way into American homes on a daily, biweekly, or weekly basis and may be exposed to an entire family. Newspapers utilized as media reach many people. Again considering specialization, individuals have certain sections of the newspaper that appeal to them—government, sports, entertainment, community activities, and business, to name a few. Therefore, the public relationist must decide which section is most often read by the public in focus and utilize that section for his message.

Fliers, brochures, reports, newsletters, and *bulletins* are common media for transmitting messages. These media often do not reach a large population but are especially effective for a well-defined audience or special segment of the public. The key concept for the individual or group vested with the responsibility of public relations is to select media according to a public's interest and therein communicate the pertinent message.

Handbooks or *manuals* provide valuable and essential information and often serve as reference material. They are a must for organizational structures but do not serve a large reading public. They possibly contribute less than many other media to the public relations effort.

Vocal Communication. *Speeches* or *public speaking* provide an opportunity for an organization or institution to meet and communicate face to face with its public in central locations. This communication may be very valuable for transmitting ideas, information, or viewpoints, since interest has been indicated by attendance. For this reason, public speaking may prove more valuable as a follow-up to some other method of message transmission. Speakers bureaus can provide experts to discuss, inform, and/or interpret messages to interested groups.

Interpublic communication may provide the greatest and most valuable public relations possible. Interpublic communication means the vocal communication often referred to as the grapevine.

This form of media may be more powerful than any other single form, yet if negatively used can be very damaging. Business representatives believe, quite frankly, that the best public relations is a satisfied customer who spreads the word. When an individual praises or attacks an organization or institution, he seldom has trouble obtaining an audience. The public will often believe a spokesman who expresses no motive other than to inform.

Organizations and institutions should not depend upon this type of public relations because it develops slowly; there are no control mechanisms; and final messages are often quite different from the original. Since it is a time-honored medium that utilizes cycle communication, the public relations program should attempt to make the very best use of it.

Visual Illustrations. *Pictures, posters, graphics,* and *charts* are a few of the many illustrative media available to the public relationist. They provide instant images that may be implanted in the receivers' minds. For this reason, the illustrative materials chosen must be direct, uncomplicated, and appealing to the eye. The public relations staff should keep in mind that a black-on-white graph of a statistical analysis will probably have no lingering effect on the broad public, if noticed at all. The same information can be conveyed more meaningfully and with better results with the aid of color and originality.

Bulletin boards and *billboards* are effective ways to communicate ideas if locations are carefully selected. They have little impact if there is no intended-receiver traffic to observe their messages. A billboard or bulletin board on a deserted roadway or in an isolated hallway is of very little consequence. However, even if the desired location is found, the message must still be interesting, informative, of value, and above all, up to date. Outdated notices soon condition the public not to look; therefore, boards should be changed often and kept current.

Motion pictures, film strips, and *slides* are effective communication or public relations tools which may provide the viewer with a true-life picture. They may present people in prescribed situations reacting in the desired manner. There is a tendency for the audience to believe and be more easily influenced when the message is seen as well as heard. Initial costs are somewhat high, but the utility often offsets the capital outlay expense. Their true cost may be considered in terms of their effectiveness with the vast numbers of people who may view them.

Planned Events. *Special days, parades,* and *festivals* frequently offer the public a chance to participate in some form of entertainment while gaining a favorable attitude and developing good will. These events must, of course, be limited in number, but an organization can reap great benefits from such activities. To utilize them for public relations requires taking a leadership role, a working role, or a sponsoring role. A special day, parade, or festival should be a joyous occasion for the public and should never appear so commercial as to interfere with the spirit of pleasure. A mistake such as this could bring on negative public relations and leave the public with just the opposite of the intended fond memories of a good time associated with a particular organization or institution.

Demonstrations and *open houses* are very useful in bringing individuals into an organization to see it at work and to see how products or services are actually produced. Many businesses have begun to beautify their surroundings and assure visitors a day they will remember. Additional entertainment, special transport vehicles, and refreshments are but a few of the extras that the public enjoys.

After-hour events are used by many organizations who sponsor activities after work hours for their employees and the public as well. Churches, industrial plants, and schools are but a few which have done so. These events are most often recreational in nature, with activities ranging from basket-weaving to team sports. The central idea is to attract the public to use the equipment and facilities and understand the value of the total program. Schools also utilize athletic events, school plays, and musical events to gain public interest in their programs. Through these media, the public can see the positive aspects of programs.

Electronic Devices. The age of scientific discovery and advanced technology has brought a new era of public relations. Electronics has made it possible to communicate at great distance and speed with large populations. Modern electronic devices have made mass communication a simple matter.

Radio and *television* have a great influence on the majority of the American population. Studies have shown the vast number of American homes with radio and television devices now considered necessities. Many businesses utilize radio and television for customer enjoyment. With such large audiences, public relations programs no longer need to select the specific public; yet there is continuous research being conducted to determine the audiences that watch or listen to particular programs.

Radio and television are probably the most effective means of singular communication since they broadcast into the home, deliver the message, and reinforce that message as often as desired. It is obvious that these devices can be very effective; yet they are often misused. Therefore, the individuals responsible for planning must present themes and ideas that catch and hold the receiver's interest if important results are obtained.

Recordings and *public address systems* may prove to be effective communication tools within limited boundaries. They provide an excellent way to impart vital information to employees or to a public. Public address systems and recordings may be made mobile with little difficulty when mobility is desired. Many organizations utilize music to increase production, create a relaxed atmosphere, or foster good relationships within their walls.

THE COMMUNITY AND PUBLIC RELATIONS

There are many targets of public relations, one of which is the very important local community. Each organization and institution has a community with which to relate. Community relations, in many instances, might well be the most significant aspect of some public relations programs. Important community relationships exist whether or not an organization or institution so desires. Every effort should be made to make these positive relationships. Community relationships may be positive by chance, but they are much more likely to be constructive when properly planned and conducted.

Any organization striving to develop a successful operation or program is more likely to succeed when community support is present. There are several reasons why an institution or organization should be a good neighbor to the surrounding community and vice versa.

1. The community usually provides much of the manpower for the organization or institution to function.
2. The community can provide financial support for the undertakings of the institution or organization.
3. The community may become friendly to the organization and provide support and backing rather than resist its endeavors.
4. The community can be greatly rewarded by its local institutions and organizations.
5. The community and its organizations have a social obligation to develop a wholesome working relationship for mutual benefit.

As previously stated, planning is a prerequisite to program success. The planning phase of community relations should be shared by all those involved. This means that organizational and community public relations personnel are involved with each other and with other representatives. The planning program should have as one of its major objectives the greatest mutual benefit for both the community and the sponsoring organization or institution. Meetings should not take the form of a negotiation, but a mutual give-and-take atmosphere should exist. There are several steps worthy of consideration in the planning of community relations programs:

1. Determine the impact of the existing community relations program and the exact status of present community relationships. If there is no structured program, it is important to determine present community relationship characteristics.
2. Decide what the community relations program is to be, determine the type of relationship desired and the dominant image for which to work in the community.
3. Study and understand the community in as much detail as possible. To achieve success, what is wanted and needed must be identified.
4. Develop and install the program based on the best information available. The planners should have a good sense of direction and understand what might be achieved.
5. Determine the method to be used to measure success.

The individual or group delegated the responsibility for developing and maintaining a sound program of community relations has to be well versed in the community's characteristics. There are many characteristics existing under the surface of community life which may only be observed and understood through close association. The following are some of the many important characteristics to be considered:

1. *Patterns of Community Response.* There are many ways a community may respond favorably or unfavorably to a community relations program. The range of community response might be from complete acceptance to complete rejection. It is important that the community relations team be well aware of the community's response to the program. Polls, surveys, face-to-face conversation or other community actions may provide required information. These data are also facets of program evaluation.
2. *Community Leadership.* The community, like any other social group, has individuals who emerge as leaders. It is extremely important that those responsible for community relations identify community leaders. Logical places to find leaders are in government positions, where they are selected by the peo-

ple of the community or in civic organizations or agencies.

3. *Community Power Structure.* Research has proved that there exists in every community one or more power structures. These individuals or groups within the larger body actually make or strongly influence community decisions. It is of assistance to community relationists to have knowledge of the existence of such structures. Though the community relations program should be aimed at the community as a whole, working with influential people and groups is important if success is to be achieved in promoting mutual benefits for the community and the organization or institution represented.

Power structures that may exist in a community are: churches, schools, former government representatives, professional groups, interest groups, newspapers, community organizations, civil rights organizations, business executives, municipal service leaders, property holders, union officials, and welfare agencies.

The organization or institution must make every effort to utilize community resources for furthering its program. The organization may depend upon the community to be friendly, to supply manpower, make available public relations media, and to utilize its products or services. The community may, likewise, depend upon the organization or institution for job security, financial prosperity, and any number of other important benefits. Through the use of community public relations media, the organization or institution can obtain the circulation of the message it desires to communicate while the media profit. Such mutual support often results in strong public relations achievements.

PUBLIC RELATIONS IN EDUCATION

At one time or another the discussion of education opens up possibilities for praise or blame, dependent upon the outlook and experience of the individuals discussing its status.

There are at least three broad categories of people when grouped according to public opinion about education. There are those who view as their responsibility the promotion and development of education in the schools and colleges of the nation. In opposition, there is the large and active group, which for one reason or another, is against the advancement of education in America. In between these groups is a vast populace. Often the

benefactors of the system, they may or may not be active supporters of education, interested in the education process, or passive
to education as a function in society. From the two extremes usually come the praise for education and the strongest criticism. The
attitudes and opinions of the middle group are most likely to be
changed, and it is this group toward which public relations programs are most likely to be effective and, consequently, most often
directed. This group will probably be responsive to information
and efforts to promote better understanding of what the system
and programs are trying to achieve in society.

Educational systems should try to promote and uphold a better
way of life under existing governance. In America, education, like
most enterprises therein, is geared to a democratic approach to
the good life. This means that philosophically the system is supported by most people; yet there is a wide range of opinion on
the details of how the whole system is to function. Because of
this wide range of beliefs, public relations programs are developed
to inform and persuade the people's attitudes and opinions toward support of programs.

Education is a powerful aspect of any society. It is through
education that the whole culture, past, present, and future, is
passed from one generation to the next. This means that ideas,
philosophies, facts, and information are presented and interpreted
to the young and adults through the educational system, its programs, and its spokesmen. Education is of prime importance to
government and sometimes in nondemocratic societies the whole
process is controlled by dictators. They believe that if education
can be controlled, the philosophy and thinking of people can be
controlled. In countries throughout the world, systems often
change following revolutions to provide the kind of concepts new
governments would like the people to have. In democratic countries education, like most aspects of life, is controlled by the will
of the people. For this reason, public relations serves an important
role. Public attitude reflecting support is where the greatest
strength will be found for promoting education.

Schools and colleges are often accused of failing to establish
good public relations. This point will not be discussed here. The
more important purpose, however, is to point out that wise educational leaders are now making an effort to get the public involved
by helping them to be better informed. Leaders have found that
programs cannot truly succeed without the interest and backing
of at least some segment of the public.

Accountability is of increasing concern on many fronts. Leaders
must realize that public relations can provide the interesting, informative news and factual information needed by the public.

Interpreting the Program

To achieve the interest and support of the public for education is one of the first basic steps. There are many media appropriate for this purpose.

When large amounts of funds are sought for buildings, equipment, or new programs, for example, the public's approval of the proposed plans is vital to their achievement. It is obvious that few people can concern themselves with the many details of institutional operation since this is the responsibility of professionals. However, the public is interested in the larger picture which includes overall directions, problems, needs, quality, and costs of education.

It is important, when planning to bring about better understanding, to consider the importance of providing a continuous flow of information over an extended period of time. Many short-range projects require immediate action, but this does not eliminate the imperative need for keeping the public informed and cultivating support and understanding on a long-range basis. It is important to decide just what information the public needs to know. Resources, time, and energy will generally be limited, and decisions must be made as to where to place the emphasis and the information that will best meet the needs at the time.

There are many kinds of information the public needs to understand such as schedules, curriculum, and financing of education. Activities are a good means of attracting public attention in order to present phases of programs that are often misunderstood. Clubs, field trips, athletics, and many other activities have great importance in the overall program; yet the relationship of these activities to the curriculum as well as their importance need to be interpreted to the public.

Financial Support of Education

Most Americans are taxpayers, and certain of them support both public and private institutions. Since costs of education are extensive and constitute a heavy tax burden, the public attitude needs to be reinforced by pointing out why the costs are great and also the results which are being achieved. Continuous interpretation of educational programs and outcomes is needed to assist the public to understand that quality and value received are related to input.

Education in the past has neglected to keep the public informed about developments and improvements in methods, curriculum, and expanding activities of the system. The fact that most education is supported by public taxation must have caused leadership to direct attention toward improving programs and to fall short in public relations efforts.

This can no longer be the case with rising costs and growing interest in where the money is being spent in public as well as private institutions. Extensive efforts must be made to provide information that will keep the public fully informed about the programs being supported and the relative importance of education to the products of such programs. This is done through good public relations programs.

Communication with Parents

Education has the advantage of working with children and the daily contacts with families. Higher education has the same advantage but has less contact with parents since students do not always live at home. This does not mean that direct contacts always work positively for education. However, when programs are satisfying to young people so that they feel growth and progress, normally a positive relationship among institutions, parents, and the public is created.

There are many ways to bring parents into closer contact with the schools through their children. Many media are appropriate for this purpose. Parents clubs, parent-teachers associations, committees, parent councils, letters, and fliers bring parents in contact with institutions frequently and are among the best ways to promote understanding and support for programs. Involvement of parents and their children in institutional activities is an important channel of communication. It should be understood that the public demonstrates wide variations of interest. Therefore, any institution has many different publics. This means, if wide support and public interest is to be gained, the public relations program should be broad and make every effort to appeal to the wide range of public interests, showing concern for each public and its prospective support.

Politics, Prejudice, and Public Opinion

Public relations programs in education must take into account that politics and prejudice play important roles in public opinion. In recent decades educational institutions have become battle grounds for local, state, and national political and prejudicial interests. Educational institutions are close to public interests and traditions; therefore, backgrounds and philosophies become immediately involved when controversial issues arise. This has been the case in recent years and such issues as taxation, integration, party politics, patriotism, human rights, war, governmental involvements, community power structures, and strategies have tended to put education in a crucial political crossfire.

Prejudices are difficult to deal with in that they are usually deeply ingrained in the individual or the group. Issues of this type are numerous and often involve sectionalism, racism, federal controls, local groups, and even family conflicts. Attitudes are difficult to change and long-range efforts are necessary. Often when change from traditional beliefs occurs, individuals remain skeptical and continue to fight to oppose such change.

Public relations programs are faced with the difficult task of working with publics often preoccupied with various conflicts and, therefore, exceptional planning is necessary to attract support and avoid further problems to education.

Misconceptions about Education

It has already been pointed out that public relations programs have many limitations. In some cases where attitudes are deeply ingrained and feelings very strong, public relations efforts have varying degrees of success.

One of the important functions of public relations planning in education is to direct attention toward effecting change in misconceptions about education. Misconceptions come about by misinformation or partial information which bring misunderstandings. Often when incorrect information becomes the subject of conversation, many misconceptions may be developed by a few people in a short time. Misunderstandings, whether positively or negatively initiated, have many sources from which to originate due to the breadth of education. Attacks on philosophy, aims, purposes, goals, objectives, organization, curriculum, staff, activities, or the products of education are constant threats to the "watch dogs" of public opinion. Public relations personnel have the constant problem of researching misconceptions and misunderstandings and providing positive information to counteract them where possible.

Hopefully, positive understanding about educational programs can be developed and in the future, misconceptions, misinformation, and gossip will fall upon educated and informed ears and not be further spread to perpetuate damage to education. This constant problem of public relations must have as one of its short-range objectives, to put out "brush fires," while promoting concurrently the sounder long-range understandings of its publics.

Limitations of Public Relations

Public relations programs at best have serious limitations. Inadequate time, limited resources—both informational and financial, and lack of trained personnel limit public relations efforts and results. There are inherent limitations of a functional and psychological nature as well. The vast number of publics, diversity of interests, degree of understanding or misunderstanding, degree of open-mindedness for change, adequacy of the programs to be promoted, selection of the most appropriate media, timing, and many other factors may affect the success of public relations efforts. Other factors have been previously discussed such as motivation, aspirations, politics, and prejudices. All of these complexities tend to aggravate the problems of public relations and often establish limitations to success before the program gets under way.

Good Public Relations Must Be Earned and Deserved

One of the strongest principles of public relations is that supportive public opinion for any enterprise must be deserved. To be deserved, it must be earned. Only under this circumstance can the attitudes of individuals and publics be genuine, dependable, and long lasting. This is true in the case of education as much, if not more, than in any aspect of American life. This means that public relations personnel must develop programs for public consumption that are factual and honest and uphold the very highest traditions of professional and personal integrity. When public support is gained, the public should be assured that education is open to inspection and that there will not be discrepancy between what is said and done. Educational institutions are for the education of children, youth, and adults. The institution belongs to the people. Therefore, the public should be encouraged to participate and feel comfortable with education; its confidence should be developed, appreciated, and protected. Only then can good public relations be gained and enjoyed.

Personnel-Management Relations

Good public relations is as important among educational personnel as it is with the outside public. Education serves the total population either directly or indirectly. It requires hundreds of thousands of personnel in the professional and nonprofessional categories to provide the total manpower to function. A democratic approach by administration in personnel management is presupposed in education.

It has been noted that public relations planning should begin internally since it is important that all personnel have contributions to make and so must be considered a part of the public relations team. When it is considered that one negative attitude may destroy almost instantly what it takes much longer for many to build, the importance of total commitment on the part of the personnel involved is realized.

Personnel relations is a very important aspect of administrative responsibility. It is important to consider that due to differences in types of work, interests, and responsibilities of professional and nonprofessional employees in education, personnel relations programs must be broad and flexible. This complicates administration.

In recent years there have been rapid changes in society that affect personnel in education. Administration has had the responsibility of keeping pace with these changes. Changing working hours, discrimination, unionization, welfare, integration, and many other factors have complicated personal relationships.

Typical personnel relations programs in education include policies related to such items as personnel selection, job performance, work loads, promotion and tenure, welfare programs (sick leave, vacations, insurance, retirement, disability, leaves, etc.), pay scales and pay raises, job assignment, professional development opportunities, and rights and responsibilities, to name but a few.

Staff organization is an important consideration in personnel management. It should provide clear-cut relationships and channels of communication for all personnel. Regardless of the size of the organization or function of the staff involved, an organization plan for a system, institution, or segment of either will often clarify administrative channels.

Organization plans range from simple to complicated depending upon the size and function of the unit so organized. Usually an organizational chart for a large school system or a large institution of higher education will be complicated and involved. Segments of such plans might require further organizational breakdown. For example, colleges within a university, schools within a college, departments within a school, and divisions within a department each might require an organization plan for clarification and control.

Staff organization offers extensive opportunity for staff growth and leadership development. Formal assignment at various administrative and supervisory levels will prepare staff personnel to climb the ladder to greater responsibility and thereby satisfy the urge to develop and succeed. Such organization may provide opportunities ranging from important administrative responsibility to minor job and committee assignments.

A much less formal kind of organization is often developed by employees themselves. Usually leadership is elected, and an organizational plan and committees developed. This gives personnel the working tools for contributing to its own welfare and offers a channel of communication to administration for use when conditions warrant and when direct contact with administration is desired. The purposes for such organizations range from the desire for recreational pursuits to negotiations on salary, working conditions, and benefits.

Keeping the staff informed and involved prevents misunderstanding and misinformation. Staff personnel must be kept informed if they are to make their contribution to the total public relations program; uninformed personnel seldom make very happy employees. The public relations staff should strive to keep all personnel apprised of the organization and its objectives as well as the total plan for public relations with the publics concerned. Only when the personnel are completely informed and involved can they be expected to make a maximum contribution.

Public relations plans will seldom promote, with the same degree of emphasis, all aspects of the educational program at once. In this case, the relationships among interdepartmental groups should lead to mutual support when special promotional efforts are under way.

Staff-community relations and involvements normally produce respected citizens who perform many functions of leadership in the community and in various civic organizations. They are usually in a good position, if well informed, to interpret education to their fellow citizens and to the groups to which they belong. This is an important public relations function, and it should be performed in a manner that is respected by the public. Association on a personal basis with friends and fellow citizens provides an extremely important means of communication with the public and makes possible an ambassadorship for education.

PUBLIC RELATIONS IN HEALTH, PHYSICAL EDUCATION, AND RECREATION

Education is a costly business. The same can be said for most phases of education. Health, physical education, and recreation are not exceptions. Education with its vastness and high costs requires a large portion of local and state budgets. In turn, health, physical education, and recreation, because of their many facets and extensive needs for faculty, indoor and outdoor spaces, costly equipment and supplies, often are among the more expensive phases of education. For this reason, the problem of interpreting the total program to secure the approval and support of students, faculties, administrators, and publics makes public relations necessary and important. As much or more than other subject areas, health, physical education, and recreation must be concerned with quality and effectiveness, as judged by laymen and professionals, when competing for public or private financing.

As previously pointed out, the public does not fully understand the education process nor the high costs of education. Unfortunately, education is often judged from the standpoint of dollars spent rather than its value to its recipients, quality of life, or the importance of an educated citizenry.

It must also be noted that, in general, students, faculties, administrators, and the public rarely understand the aims and objectives, curriculum and noncurriculum activities, potential achievements, or ultimate goals of health, physical education and recreation. Therefore, interpretation and salesmanship are necessary to achieve understanding, interest, approval, and support. This is the important role of public relations, whether promoted by chance or through planned programs. However, to achieve sufficient understanding and support, planned programs must, by necessity, become a reality and must be continuous.

Present programs need to be supported, expanded, and new programs developed to provide adequately for oncoming populations. This is a difficult responsibility. It is imperative that professionals and student professionals dedicate themselves to the tasks of developing quality programs and more effective ways of interpreting them for all consumers. The learning experiences to achieve these goals deserve an important place in the professional preparation of student professionals.

Program Planning

There are many ways to plan and conduct public relations programs. Plans and details should be based upon intensive study and research. Sound principles should be employed and programs should be conducted with honesty and integrity. Public relations programs should take a long-range approach unless in response to immediate crises. Plans must reflect concern for the public as well as for the institution. A cooperative spirit and attitude must be achieved within the institution and should be cultivated throughout the publics involved. Success should be deserved and appreciated.

Identification of Publics

One of the early considerations in public relations planning is to identify individuals and groups of individuals toward whom programs may be directed. The idea, of course, is to cultivate support for all programs, and therefore, many publics may be involved. When the total program including health, physical education, and recreation is considered, it may well touch the largest general public of all education. Some publics may be negative or even hostile to particular programs. These publics are much more difficult to change in the direction of support and should have special attention. Wider acceptance may be achieved through better understanding of program objectives and results.

Publics of great importance to health, physical education, and recreation are: students, faculty members, administrators, alumni, school board members, parents, laymen, special interest groups, agencies, clubs, organizations, and businesses. The goal to help individuals and groups feel a close tie with the institution and develop pride and spirit in its accomplishments ultimately brings backing and support.

Cultivating Public Interest

Every effort should be made to build upon and develop interest which might be manifested in a very minor way. Each program area and activity has a potential public. When many publics, even though small, are combined they might well become a large population capable of major support. This should be a very real strength since there there are so many programs, activities, and sports involved in the total program. It must be understood that the responsibility for public relations for health, physical education and recreation rests therein and cannot be left for some other educational area to provide. Publics should be kept well informed, respected as partners in an important undertaking, and appreciated for their interest and support.

Keys to Interest and Support

1. Sending home satisfied customers is one of the best forms of public relations. When experiences are good and growth is achieved, students at any level seem to have a way of knowing it and their satisfaction is expressed. Faculty should make every effort to conduct class instruction and other activities in such meaningful and productive ways as to assure that students, feeling a sense of growth and improvement, look forward to the next class or activity. When this is the case, favorable results are forthcoming, and such programs become indispensable to the school, college, and community.
2. Program development and improvement is a very important factor. Research findings should be a key to curriculum development, and revision and learning experiences provided should be relevant to the beliefs of students, faculty, and public. Programs and activities should be broad enough to meet the

needs and interests of all students, at all levels, in school and college. Parents are most likely to support programs and institutions if their sons and daughters are happy, involved, and learning. Initiative and creativeness in updating programs are important and appreciated. The assurance that adequate libraries, instructional methods and materials, faculties, and facilities are desired and sought stimulates pride and initates favorable response. Activities that involve all students, such as intramurals, capture the interest of parents whose children are not especially gifted in athletic activities. Programs for the faculty and the public under good leadership aid understanding among important groups.

3. Emphasizing important interests and trends which apply to health, physical education, and recreation during any period demonstrates that professionals are knowledgeable, abreast of the issues, and sensitive to the interests and needs of the times. These interests and concerns may be worked into the course of study or, if more appropriate, approached through activities of selected types.

4. Cooperation with community groups in sponsoring programs, providing leadership, and making facilities available are extensions of public relations and usually cultivate the goodwill and support of the public.

5. A display of programs through the involvement of students gains interest and support. Most people are interested in seeing students perform. This is very true of parents, many of whom do not often have the opportunity to witness such participation by their children.

6. The quality of programs and activities is largely dependent upon the strength of the faculty. The public takes justifiable pride in the confidence it enjoys when it believes in the faculty and what it is doing for the students. Involvement of the public in the various programs is much less difficult when under sound leadership.

7. Public relations is enhanced when human relations is involved. Person-to-person or one-to-one contact is the strongest arm of public relations. Humanizing learning experiences, whether in the classroom or in other activities, develops strong personal relationships with students and the public. This type of

public relations should be practiced to the maximum.

8. Positive thinking, confidence, and demonstration of ability are attractive to students, colleagues, and the public. A negative attitude is detrimental. Confidence in the profession, its aims, objectives, and capabilities for achieving results is a winning attitude of great importance. This attitude is appreciated by adversaries and electrifying to supporters. Furthermore, such attitude gives proof that professionals believe in what they are doing.

9. The image of health, physical education, and recreation is improved when quality programs, quality leadership, and quality results are on display for public review.

10. Programs and activities must be interpreted to the public in the full depth and breadth of their purpose. Values and results must be explained and interpreted. Through this effort the public really knows what is being done and why. It takes an unusual individual to withhold support when the why of health, physical education, recreation, and athletics is fully understood.

11. Honesty and sincerity are important avenues to friendship and confidence. Overselling is dangerous, and misrepresentation of the facts is unnecessary and destructive to good relationships. One individual who is careless, intellectually or professionally dishonest, or unwilling to make his contribution may well become an unbearable burden to public relations.

12. Support gained at any level must be earned and deserved. It should be appreciated, used with care, and cultivated on a long-range basis.

13. Evaluation of the public relations program is very important. The finest tools of evaluation, appropriate to the situation, should be employed. Evaluation should be continuous. Public relations plans might require adjustment in light of evaluated results.

Important Media

Health, physical education, and recreation programs lend themselves well to many publicity media. All appropriate media resources should be used to the maximum.

The *press, television,* and *radio* are excellent media for publicizing and presenting the program and activities to the public; however, a great deal of cooperation is necessary. Writing and delivering properly prepared releases and announcements to the media usually get good results and are often necessary. Meeting media deadlines is important. Providing the necessary basic arrangements for these media at games and other activities to be covered, is an institutional responsibility.

Demonstrations, clinics, instructional sessions, and *workshops* are important public relations media. These activities give opportunity to display programs involving many people, and they attract much interest. Many aspects of the program can be displayed in this way. Gymnastics, dance, wrestling, swimming, and other sports not often observed by the public may be presented in this manner to large audiences.

Brochures, fliers, posters, bulletin boards, newsletters, and *campus newspapers* may be distributed to homes throughout the community and to distant publics to interpret programs, make announcements, give schedules, and extend invitations to institutional activities.

Athletic games and *contests* lend themselves easily to the use of many media while they too are good for public relations. They bring together large groups of supporters and provide major opportunities for the extension of public understanding. Game programs and brochures often contain information about the institution and its academic programs. This too is important public relations.

EVALUATION IN PUBLIC RELATIONS

A public relations program, like any other program, must follow an operational cycle of which evaluation is a part. This is a very important part of the cycle since only evaluation can answer the question: are objectives being met? Diagram 3 illustrates the operational cycle. This cycle is, perhaps, oversimplified, but it is operational and basic to any undertaking. The cycle does not end with

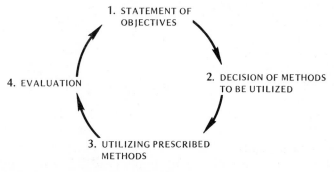

Diagram 3 OPERATIONAL CYCLE

evaluation, for it is a continuous process. Evaluation can ultimately tell whether or not objectives are achievable, if methods selected are adequate, and if there is effective utilization of these methods.

If evaluation is to function, there must be some yardstick by which success in public relations can be measured. Some business organizations view the profit margin column to determine the success or failure of public relations. A politician counts his votes to visualize the impact of public relations. An institution of higher education might well look to the enrollment figures to gain some insight about its public relations. These appear well and good on the surface but they do not give a clear, concise, factual picture of what the public relations program has or has not achieved.

To evaluate a public relations program, one must take into account the many variables that come into play. These are intangible and unpredictable items that include public attitude and reaction. It is, therefore, important to strive to develop more precise instruments, or yardsticks, to adequately gauge the true impact of public relations. If at first the public relations program is not realizing the desired objectives, hope should not be abandoned. Likewise, a good public relations program is not content with only reaching established objectives. A good program continuously extends its objectives and asks itself to answer much more difficult questions.

The plan of evaluation should be continuous, varied, and useful. Evaluation is not conducted just for the sake of evaluation, but for overall program improvement. Evaluation should involve everyone who is in any way a part of the total program and not just the public relations staff. Each staff member and employee should play some role in evaluation and should be made aware of the results. Each should then be a part of implementing any new program changes resulting. Evaluation is the process of employing all available tools and devices of measurement in contrasting the objectives sought with the results obtained. The type of research employed and the tools of measurement used will depend upon the nature of the program and procedures used.

With an emphasis on accountability, programs must be evaluated adequately and demonstrate their value if they are to be worthy of continued existence. Especially in times of high operational costs, all programs must look for new ways to show their real values. It is, therefore, important that institutions develop or strengthen their public relations program and that public relationists seek to strengthen their procedures for improving services to their publics.

In the final chapter, entitled "Evaluating the Administrator," Dr. Shenk discusses ways in which the administrator's effectiveness

NOTES

[1] Howard Stephenson, ed., *Handbook of Public Relations,* 2d ed. (New York: McGraw-Hill Book Company, 1971), p. 8.
[2] Philip Lesly, ed., *Public Relations Handbook,* 3d ed. (Englewood Cliffs, N.J.: Prentice-Hall, 1967), p. 395.
[3] Lesly, *Public Relations Handbook,* p. 886.
[4] Ibid.
[5] Scott M. Cutlip and Allen H. Center, *Effective Public Relations,* 3d ed. (Englewood Cliffs, N.J.: Prentice-Hall, 1964), p. 70.
[6] Stephenson, *Handbook of Public Relations,* p. 8.
[7] Cutlip and Center, *Effective Public Relations,* p. 135.
[8] Nugent Wedding, "Public Relations in Business," *University of Illinois Bulletin,* vol. 47 (July, 1950), p. 32.
[9] Gordon McCloskey, *Education and Public Understanding,* 2d ed. (New York: Harper and Row, Publishers, 1967), pp. 66-7.

BIBLIOGRAPHY

Books

Bloomberg, Warner, Jr. and Sunshine, Morris. *Suburban Power Structures and Public Relations.* Syracuse, N.Y.: Syracuse University Press, 1964.

Brownell, Clifford Lee; Gans, Leo; and Maroon, Tufie Z. *Public Relations in Education.* New York: McGraw-Hill Book Co., 1955.

Bucher, Charles A. *Administration of School and College Health and Physical Education Programs.* 4th ed. St. Louis: The C. V. Mosby Co., 1967.

Canfield, Bertrand, R. *Public Relations Principles, Cases, and Problems.* 5th ed. Homewood, Ill.: Richard D. Irwin, 1968.

Cratty, William J. *Public Opinion and Politics: A Reader.* New York: Holt, Rinehart and Winston, 1970.

Daugherty, Grayson and Woods, John B. *Physical Education Programs: Organization and Administration.* Philadelphia: W. B. Saunders Co., 1971.

DeFleur, Melvin L. *Theories of Mass Communications.* 2d ed. New York: David McKay Co., 1970.

Dover, C. J. *Management Communications on Controversial Issues.* Washington, D.C.: BNA Incorporated, 1965.

Ferry, W. H. and Ashmore, Harry S. *Mass Communications.* New York: The Fund for the Republic, 1966.

George, Jack F. and Lehman, Harry A. *School Athletic Administration.* New York: Harper and Row Publishers, 1966.

Golden, Hal and Hanson, Kitty. *How to Plan, Produce, and Publicize Special Events.* New York: Oceana Publications, 1960.

Haselden, Kyle. *Morality and the Mass Media.* Nashville: Broadman Press, 1968.

Hennessy, Bernard C. *Public Opinion.* Belmont, Calif.: Wadsworth Publishing Co., 1965.

Hughes, William Leonard; French, Esther; and Lehsten, Nelson G. *Administration of Physical Education for Schools and Colleges.* New York: The Ronald Press Co., 1962.

Jones, James T. *School Public Relations.* New York: The Center for Applied Research in Education, 1966.

Kindred, Leslie W. *How to Tell the School Story.* Englewood Cliffs, N.J.: Prentice-Hall, 1960.

Lee, John, ed. *The Democratic Persuaders New Role of the Mass Media in International Relations.* New York: John Wiley and Sons, 1968.

Marston, John E. *The Nature of Public Relations.* New York: McGraw-Hill Book Co., 1963.

Roolman, Arthur R. *Profitable Public Relations.* Homewood, Ill.: Dow Jones-Irwin, 1968.

Schoenfeld, Clarence A. *Publicity Media and Methods.* New York: The Macmillan Company, 1963.

Voltmer, Edward F. and Esslinger, Arthur A. *The Organization and Administration of Physical Education.* 4th ed. New York: Appleton-Century-Crofts, 1967.

Zeigler, Earle F. *Administration of Physical Education and Athletics.* Englewood Cliffs, N.J.: Prentice-Hall, 1959.

Periodicals

Allen, W. S. "Does P. R. Need Redefinition?" *Public Relations Journal* 26 (July, 1970): 23-24.

Aszling, R. A. "Consumerism and the P.R. Response." *Public Relations Journal* 26 (October, 1970): 89-90.

Bateman, J. Carroll. "The Tomorrow Factor in P. R." *Public Relations Quarterly* 16 (1971): 14.

Biles, Fay. "P E P I." *Journal of Health, Physical Education, and Recreation* 42 (September, 1971): 53-55.

Celtnieks, Vince. "School Public Relations." *Journal of Health, Physical Education, and Recreation* 40 (November–December, 1969): 82.

Cunningham, Lavern L. "Community Involvement in Change." *Educational Leadership* 27 (January, 1970): 363.

Dowell, Linus. "Physical Education: Practice, Public Opinion and Presumption." *Physical Educator* 24 (May, 1967): 79-81.

Ford, H. "Revolution in Public Expectations." *Public Relations Journal* 26 (October, 1970): 16-18.

Fujita, S. N. "Design Fortifies the Message." *Public Relations Journal* 26 (October, 1970): 98-99.

"Imagemakers Fight Their Own Image." *Industry Week* 166 (June, 1970): 40-43.

Kean, G. "Importance of International Public Relations." *California Management Review* 13 (Summer, 1971): 68-78.

Leibrock, Philip J. "Intramural Publicity and P. R." *Physical Educator* 22 (October, 1965): 105-106.

Lesly, Phillip. "Changing Media: A Challenge to P. R." *Public Relations Journal* 26 (May, 1970): 20-21.

"National Conference on International Relations Through H P E R." *Journal of Health, Physical Education and Recreation* 38 (September, 1967): 10-12.

Newman, Ian. "School and Community Relations." *School Health Review* 2 (November, 1971): 16.

Nightengale, Earl. "How Will Today's Physical Education Be Remembered in 1989?" *Journal of Health, Physical Education, and Recreation* 40 (February, 1969): 42.

Nulton, John E. "We Are On Display." *Journal of Health, Physical Education, and Recreation* 34 (April, 1963): 27.

Roth, J. A. "New Patterns in Community Leadership." *Public Relations Journal* 26 (June, 1970): 22-23.

Rice, Arthur H. "Schools Must Revamp Their Public Relations Program." *Nation's School* 83 (April, 1969): 14-16.

Roper, Elmo. "Reaching the General Public." *Public Relations Quarterly* 16 (1971).

Sandberg. R. A. "New Roles For Public Relations Managers." *Public Relations Journal* 26 (October, 1970): 101-102.

Shaw, R. "P. R. Training for Para-Professionals." *Public Relations Journal* 26 (November, 1970): 16-19.

Singer, Robert N. "Communicate or Perish." *Journal of Health, Physical Education, and Recreation* 39 (February, 1968): 40-41.

Torpey, James. "Interpreting Physical Education for the Public." *Physical Educator* 24 (October, 1967): 131.

"The School Public Relations Administrator." *NEA Research Bulletin* 46 (March, 1968).

chapter 6

Evaluating
The Administrator

HENRY SHENK

Administration is essentially concerned with setting up a program and seeing that all of the available resources are so managed as to make the program effective. It involves the management of human beings. As Miller points out,

> Administration is a broadly conceived term including the whole process of decision making and action taking—under such a view the professional administration staff is concerned both with policy development and enactment and with carrying out the policies enacted.[1]

The administrator of a department is the person who is given the responsibility for organizing or managing the department. He is entrusted with certain executive or administrative powers and is ultimately held responsible for the proper functioning of the department. From time to time the administrator is evaluated.

Evaluating the administrator is no easy task. Formal evaluation always involves value judgments about how effective an administrator has been in achieving departmental goals. There are always going to be evaluations of the administration whether the conclusions reached are justifiable or not. It is essential that the formal evaluation of an administrator is made on the basis of facts and that the conclusions reached as a result of the evaluation will be fair both to the administrator and to the school system. As pointed out by Morphet and his colleagues:

> Appraisals are inevitable . . . The question that confronts the educational administrator, therefore, is not whether there will be appraisals. It is rather whether or not the appraisals will be reasonably valid or only judgments made on the basis of inadequate data or even with merely rumor as the "foundation."[2]

The school or departmental administrator in higher education is primarily an educator, and his business is education. At the risk of oversimplification, the educational process consists of three parts: (1) determination of the goals to be achieved; (2) interaction between students and teachers to achieve these goals; and (3) an evaluation of the results.

A parallel might be drawn between education and the automobile industry. In the latter, (1) the goal is to build high quality automobiles at a price the public will pay; (2) by proper interaction of superior workmen with high quality materials, the finished automobile is produced; and (3) this product is then given repeated tests, and the final evaluation is made by the public on how well the car performs. If the public likes the product, many cars are sold and the industry flourishes. Management plays a most important part in the auto industry because of the vital importance of wise decisions and sound policies. Not only is the product evaluated but management, too, is constantly being judged as to its effectiveness. In the business of education, management plays an equally important role.

Just as the final evaluation of cars rests with the public, so does society appraise the effectiveness of the educational process. The chief executive of an automobile industry is a key figure in determining the quality of the final product, as is the department chairman (or dean) in determining the end product of education. Because of the importance of the administrator in determining the quality of education, it is even more necessary that he be evaluated just as the managers of industry are periodically evaluated.

The importance of the administrator's role in producing quality graduates cannot be overestimated. He helps to develop programs and policies and is responsible for seeing that decisions reached and policies established are properly administered. He is called upon to make decisions on many matters, some of which are controversial. His ability to make wise decisions and to work harmoniously with people determines his success as an administrator.

Four questions may be raised about evaluating the administrator:

1. What types of departmental evaluation are there?

2. Who makes the evaluation?
3. What qualities of the administrator are evaluated?
4. What uses are made of the results of the evaluation?

WHAT TYPES OF DEPARTMENTAL EVALUATION ARE THERE?

There are two general types of departmental evaluation. The first is *informal* evaluation and the second, *formal*. Both are important for successful and efficient administration. Informal evaluation or appraisal is constantly taking place. Formal evaluation of a department or a school takes place only at specified times and usually in response to some felt or expressed need. When a department or school is evaluated, the administrator is invariably evaluated, too, since the administrator must accept ultimate responsibility for the success or failure or the operation.

Informal Evaluations

A great many people make informal judgments about the physical education administrator. The administrator of a college department of physical education, by the nature of his position, has more tasks to perform, more responsibilities to accept, more contacts with the publics than do department chairmen of many other academic disciplines. In addition to the duties the physical education chairman shares with other department chairmen, he must also help to develop and enforce policies and make administrative decisions about such diverse problems as the use of physical education and recreation facilities, intramural programs, intercollegiate programs, extramural athletics, recreational programs, and faculty recreation. The physical education administrator has many opportunities for coming into personal contact with students and faculty who invariably make appraisals of the administrator and value judgments about the program and the management of the department.

Each person who has contact with an administrator, either consciously or unconsciously makes some sort of judgment about him. Each "satisfied customer" becomes a booster for the department; those with bad impressions or experiences become severe critics or even enemies. With favorable experiences the department status is enhanced; with unfavorable reactions, the entire program may be placed in jeopardy or destroyed.

There are essentially four different groups who come in contact with the administrator, his policies, and program, and with whom he must have good rapport if he is to be evaluated highly and his administration is to be successful. These groups are (1) the students, (2) colleagues in his department and in the institution, (3) his administration superiors, and finally (4) members of the various publics outside of the education institution. Each of these groups will be considered in turn.

Students. Students not only are important but are the sine qua non in any educational program. How much they come in contact with the administrator depends upon his accessibility. Some administrators have an open door policy and see students at almost any time, even at the expense of sacrificing time that could be profitably spent in other administrative activities. Other administrators make themselves almost inaccessible to students. Students rarely see these chairmen except in cases of dire emergency. Administrators who teach classes are at least known by students. However, whether students know the administrator or not, they constantly evaluate the departmental operation.

Policies developed by the staff and implemented by the department chairman or dean also affect students either favorably or unfavorably. If students consider policies unfair, oppressive, or unwarranted, the administrator is blamed. Good public relations and communication with students are essential for good administration. Mutual trust and respect among students, faculty, and administration must prevail if a program is to reach its optimum potential. An administrator who has earned the confidence and goodwill of the students, through their informal evaluations, has laid the groundwork for successful administration.

Colleagues in the Department. The approval of one's departmental colleagues is also important for successful administration. In the countless contacts that administrators have with staff members, evaluation takes place: staff meetings, informal settings, social situations. The administrator is judged on his development of policies, enforcement of regulations, and consistency of behavior. It is absolutely essential that the administrator deal fairly with his colleagues and that he be impartial in his treatment of staff members. If administration is carried on through the democratic process; if staff members share in policy-making decisions; if each person is made to feel important; if each shares in program planning; and if each feels that it is his program, then the administrator will usually have staff support.

Informal appraisal by staff members affects the success of an administrator. His acceptance and even his professional long-term survival depend upon his ability to work harmoniously and fruitfully with his staff. Without staff acceptance and loyalty, a department or school cannot hope to make significant educational contributions. Individuals in the department may do so but not the department nor school as a whole.

Administrative Superiors. Superiors comprise a third group who forms opinions about the chairman. Whether these superiors are deans, presidents or vice-presidents at the collegiate level, or high school principals or superintendents at the public school level, it is important that they have a favorable impression of the physical education administrator. These impressions are acquired both through direct contacts and reports.

The wise physical education administrator makes sure that in his direct contacts with superiors, his image as an administrator is enhanced. The reports he submits should be carefully done and on time. He should attend faculty meetings and senate meetings regularly, observe the policies that have been developed, and cooperate with his immediate superior. Respecting the administrative organization, he should go through proper channels and not bypass his immediate superior. His loyalty should be unquestioned.

There are many situations in which the chairman or dean comes in contact with his superiors: in the faculty club or lounge, in corridors, on the street or on the campus, at parties, receptions, at church, at service clubs, etc. A favorable impression can result in acceptance and continued support; an unfavorable one can sometimes negate an otherwise promising career. The writer knows of one instance where a very promising young college administrator lost all opportunity for advancement by telling an inappropriate story in the presence of a college president. The college president received an entirely false image of the character of this man through this one unfortunate incident.

Administrative superiors get reports of their subordinates from a variety of sources. These reports may come from students, departmental colleagues, or the general public. If students or faculty seem to be constantly unhappy, if there are unfavorable or derogatory occurrences reported in the press, and if these instances seem to recur with considerable frequency, the administrative head is likely to begin to question his subordinate's judgment and his fitness for his position. On the other hand, if reports reaching the administrative head are favorable, the subordinate is likely to become more secure in his position or even be promoted to a position of greater responsibility.

The Publics. Outside of the educational institution there are many publics with whom the physical education administrator has contact. They, too, make informal evaluations. Among these are the news media, parents, alumni, local schools, local clubs, churches, chambers of commerce, and merchants. While their judgments may not carry much weight with governing bodies, good public relations with them is always a plus for an administrator. A critical letter from an irate parent or alumnus, a critical or damaging article by writers in the local paper, or hostility of religious or civic groups can sometimes do great harm to a physical education department and its administration. While it may be necessary in the enforcement of departmental policies to cross some of these groups, the wise chairman takes time to explain the reasons for the policies and decisions and makes every effort to preserve good public relations, meanwhile exhibiting firmness as well as fairness.

Formal Evaluations

In addition to the informal evaluations made by various groups, formal evaluations are set up at intervals to appraise the department's effectiveness in producing quality education. A judgment is made not only about the departmental operation but also about the departmental chairman. It is inescapable that he be evaluated along with his school or department. Seldom does a program become good without superior leadership; the converse is not always true. A poor program may be due to factors beyond the administrator's control; yet he cannot escape responsibility.

There are at least three ways in which a department may be formally evaluated: (1) by self-evaluation, (2) by accrediting agencies, and (3) by a committee formed for this purpose.

Self-evaluation. One of the most important types of formal evaluation is self-evaluation. Self-evaluation may be done by the department as a means of improving the program, or it may be done as a step prior to a visit by an accrediting body. As a tool that the wise administrator uses to improve the program, self-evaluation makes individual faculty members more knowledgeable about the philosophy of the department, its objectives, its organization, its policies, its strengths, and its weaknesses. It serves not only as a good means of providing information for action but also it is an excellent means of in-service training.

Accrediting Agencies. In most states the state departments of education are charged with evaluating schools of education and, in the process, evaluate and accredit their component departments. State departments too are almost invariably represented on other accreditation teams from outside the state. It is doubtful that a department or school could be accredited by any agency without first being accredited by its own state department of education. The state department may call upon colleagues from the public schools or other colleges within the state to assist them in this task.

A university or college usually is rated by the appropriate regional accrediting agency. This is ordinarily done at periodic intervals. Approval and accreditation by the regional association is much sought after and implies that the institution has at least met minimal standards.

A third accrediting body is the National Council for the Accreditation of Teacher Education (NCATE). This group periodically visits and accredits departments or schools of education (including physical education when it is located in education). Accreditation by any of these three accrediting agencies indicates that a judgment has been made and that the department and its program have met the standards required by the accrediting group.

Evaluation by a Committee. Another type of department or school evaluation is done internally by a committee selected for this purpose. Members of the committee may come from the department being evaluated or from other departments within the college or university. Each college or university develops its own criteria for evaluation and for membership on the committee. Many times, students are included on the committee.

Still another method of evaluating a department is to bring in a team of experts from a professional organization such as AAHPER (American Association for Health, Physical Education & Recreation) or NCPEAM (National College Physical Education Association for Men). The evaluative team is made up of a few handpicked experts in the field who are considered qualified by reason of long experience and recognized competence. Such visitations may come at the instigation of the department, the chairman, the dean, or the president of the institution. The findings of a visiting team invariably either strengthens or weakens the administrator's position.

WHAT QUALITIES OF THE ADMINISTRATOR ARE EVALUATED?

In the preceding material, attention was paid to the various groups that make evaluations or appraisals. Attention will now be turned to those qualities of the administrator that may be evaluated either formally or informally, among which are personal qualities and administrative abilities. Personal qualities include: (1) personal appearance, (2) health and fitness, (3) articulateness, (4) reliability, (5) integrity, (6) sensitivity, (7) judgment, (8) ability to get along with people, (9) breadth of knowledge and intelligence, (10) vision, (11) creativeness, and (12) leadership.

Personal Qualities

Personal Appearance. The administrator should present himself as favorably as possible. Cleanliness, neatness, good grooming, and appropriate dress are important to the acceptance of an administrator by his colleagues and students. Extremes in dress and grooming should be avoided. While other qualities are much more important, a favorable impression is always a decided asset.

Health and Fitness. An administrator of a physical education department should be an example of what the physical education profession advocates—good health and optimum physical fitness.

A person who is excessively overweight or obviously in poor health adds little to the professional image of either himself or the department. Furthermore, a person who is chronically ill does not have the energy nor stamina to meet the many problems with which the physical education administrator is constantly besieged. Reasonably good physical and mental health is essential for efficient administration. Physical fitness should and can be attained by most physical educators through proper attention to exercise, nutrition, rest, and the elimination of strains and stresses. Health and fitness is one area where it is fairly easy to make an evaluation of the status of the administrator.

Articulateness. The ability to speak (and write) fluently is a tremendous asset. A facility with words and a good command of the language enable the administrator to communicate effectively. It is sometimes the case that an individual uses English correctly but is not very articulate and consequently does not communicate well. Final judgment must include not only what he *says* but what he *does*.

Reliability. This quality is most essential. The reliable administrator can be depended upon with complete confidence. His behavior and judgment are predictable: his colleagues can be sure that under certain circumstances he will react in certain ways. He can be counted upon to uphold the policies and principles on which his department operates. When administrators are inconsistent and unpredictable, confusion and distrust develop.

Integrity. Integrity is closely associated with reliability. However, there is an important difference. Integrity implies honesty, uprightness, and consistently good behavior. It means the adherence to high ideals and high moral standards. Alone, reliability may not be an admirable characteristic. For example, a person could be reliable in that he predictably exhibits antisocial or immoral behavior, but he could hardly be said to have integrity. Everyone has a right to expect that the head of a department have a high degree of integrity as well as reliability.

Sensitivity. This quality is a decided asset. It implies an awareness of other people's problems and the ability to empathize. A sensitivity to the impact that new decisions and new policies have on other people often averts personnel problems before they appear. Voltmer and Esslinger state that "the crux of administration is managing human behavior."[3] Sensitivity is crucial if the administrator is to obtain the good will of his staff, the students, and his superiors.

Judgment. The ability to make wise decisions and to take sound courses of action is embodied in the term *judgment*—sometimes referred to as good common sense or horse sense. Since the department head or dean constantly makes administrative decisions, good judgment must be exercised not only in making those choices, but also in carrying out policies. In fact, a person is usually chosen for this position of authority because it is expected that he will make wise and considered judgments. His actions, too, must reflect mature judgment and good common sense.

The administrator of physical education must learn to put first things first; he must develop a system of priorities. Since human values take precedence over material things, therefore good judgment indicates that the education and welfare of the student be given top priority. Policies and decisions that further the educational goals of the department must take precedence over personal aims or individual considerations.

One indication of good judgment is loyalty to one's superiors, colleagues, profession, and the institution in which he works. This does not mean that the administrator will never differ with his colleagues or his superiors. But it does mean that after a course of action has been chosen, he will follow that course, even if it differs with his private views. Disloyalty and poor judgment are reasons why many persons in authority fail.

The Ability to Get Along with People. This trait is necessary for the successful administrator. It does not mean that the administrator never says no or that he always gives everyone what is wanted. It does mean that he makes a real effort to be pleasant and agreeable and to avoid antagonizing persons unnecessarily. The wise chairman or dean considers himself a member of the team and works shoulder to shoulder with his colleagues in a common cause. He does not assign tasks that he himself would not be willing to do.

Cheerfulness, friendliness, a ready smile, and a good sense of humor are attributes that help anyone. In evaluating the administrator, the ability to get along with people ranks as one of the most important considerations.

Breadth of Knowledge and Intelligence. The administrator has to be knowledgeable in his field. Ordinarily he should possess the terminal degree if he works at the college level and at least the master's degree if he is a supervisor or director of programs below the collegiate level. Not only should the head of the program know a great deal about each specialized area in his field but should have a good general education and be well informed in disciplines other than his own. The alert and professional chairman or dean should keep abreast of current thinking and programs by attending conventions and participating in professional meetings. He needs to read widely and be familiar with current literature, not only in physical education, but the related areas of health, recreation, and safety.

Vision. Closely related to knowledge is the ability to think big and see "the big picture," educationally speaking. The administrator must be a dreamer, but he must combine vision with practicality if an innovative program is to result. The wise administrator is constantly thinking ahead and setting up goals and plans for the future. He must be able to see, better than others, the total effect of decisions and policies upon the total program for ten or twenty-five years into the future. The possession of vision is a trait difficult to evaluate, but it is very important.

Creativity. If vision and creative ability can be combined with practicality, an administrator should be able to develop a progressive, functioning program. New ideas should be constantly evaluated. Change is desirable if it is worthwhile. Creative ability, if not personally possessed, can at least be encouraged among staff members. While not absolutely essential, creativity is a decided asset if progress is to be made.

Leadership. An administrator can be merely a presiding officer at departmental meetings, a chore boy, or he can furnish dynamic leadership. How well a department or school functions is dependent to a large measure on the vision, the judgment, the industry, the creativity, and the administrative ability of the leader.

The preceding twelve traits are not all-inclusive but suggest qualities that are being evaluated informally and sometimes formally by those persons with whom the administrator comes into contact.

Administrative Abilities

The administrator is also judged and evaluated on his utilization of administrative skills. This evaluation too, may be either formal or informal. Among these skills are (1) the ability to delegate authority; (2) the ability to clearly indicate the staff relationships and organizational structure; (3) the ability for office management; (4) the ability to develop and control the budget; (5) the ability to recruit able staff members and maintain good staff morale; and (6) the ability to attract funds for research.

The Ability to Delegate Authority. It is obvious that the larger an administrative unit becomes, the more necessary it is to delegate authority. The ability of the head of an administrative unit, whether he be a college president, superintendent of schools, dean, principal or department chairman, to obtain good subordinates and then delegate responsibility to them is the mark of a good administrator. Since a program is only as good as the subordinates make it, the effectiveness and success of an administrator rests to a very large degree upon his obtaining able subordinates, and receiving the cooperation, loyalty, and interest of those to whom authority has been delegated. Most people like to be members of the team. They like the extra status that the delegation of authority gives them. The good administrator uses this device to develop a better staff morale.

The Ability to Clearly Indicate the Staff Relationships and Organizational Structure. This principle is very important. There should be a clear understanding as to whom a subordinate reports. No one should have more than one boss. Line-staff relationships must be crystal clear. One of the most difficult problems arises when the subordinate bypasses his immediate superior and carries problems to a higher authority. The staff member who refuses to take no for an answer and attempts to circumvent the chairman by taking the problem to the dean or to the president, not only indicates a lack of respect for the chairman, but also places the chairman in an untenable position. There is no surer evidence of lack of respect than that of bypassing immediate supervisors on important matters. Colleagues and students soon realize where the power lies. While no modern educator would want the formal chain of command used by the military, some organizational structure of the department is necessary.

This organizational structure is evaluated informally and is always a consideration in formal evaluations.

The Ability for Office Management. The efficient management of an office is of itself an indication of administrative skill. The only contact many people have with a department is with office personnel, secretaries, typists, receptionists, and others. Pleasant, courteous, efficient, and friendly secretaries give favorable impressions to visitors to the department. Conversely, probably nothing creates a more unfavorable reaction than a secretary who ignores a visitor, who is insolent, discourteous, or inefficient.

The administrator has a responsibility to see that the office is run efficiently, that reports are prepared on time and neatly typed, that records are kept accurately, and that an adequate filing system is maintained. Reasonableness, fairness, friendliness, and considerateness on the part of the chairman improve office morale and develop an esprit de corps essential to a well-run department. If the department head can instill the office staff with the feeling that each is a member of the team or an important cog in the departmental operation, he can expect loyalty in return. An equal distribution of the secretarial work load goes far in eliminating tensions and frictions that sometimes are detrimental to efficient functioning of a department. It is in the area of office management that so many informal evaluations of the administrator take place.

The Ability to Develop and Control the Budget. Obtaining adequate funds to operate a department or school is never easy and in recent years has become much more difficult. All school administrators have been finding the adequate financing of their schools or departments a big problem. Not only must the department head try to secure adequate funds, but he is frequently held responsible when the funds are not forthcoming. How well he is able to secure the funds to pay salaries that attract an able faculty and secure adequate facilities, supplies, and equipment will have a bearing on how well the department functions and how good the program really is.

Not only must the chairman try to obtain the best financial support possible, but once the budget is established, his administration of the budget and his control of the budget are perhaps the most vital parts of administration. To some extent the physical education program can be controlled by the wise use of the budget. The direction the department takes is determined to a great degree by the allocation of funds for various enterprises within the department.

The Ability to Recruit Able Staff Members and Maintain Good Staff Morale. Though many times the recruitment of good staff members is closely tied in with the amount of money available for salaries, some administrators seem to possess the knack of being able to recognize and recruit outstanding individuals while others seem invariably to recruit the wrong persons. One of the greatest assets that an administrator can have is the ability to recruit and keep high-quality staff members. The maintenance of good staff morale, along with bringing in new staff members of high quality, almost ensures a fine department.

The Ability to Attract Funds for Research. Along with the ability of the department chairman to acquire funds from the general college budget for the use of the department, he must make every effort to acquire research grants from private enterprise and from government sources. This is particularly true if the department is to be active in research and in graduate work. He should encourage young staff members to seek research grants and should help them in the acquisition of funds from all legitimate sources.

WHAT USES ARE MADE OF THE EVALUATION?

The administrator is evaluated for a variety of reasons. The evaluation may be a routine, perfunctory, periodic evaluation; it may be undertaken to improve the department and the administration; it may be undertaken because of faculty or student unrest and complaints; or it may be undertaken with the possibility that the department head be replaced or removed.

More and more frequently, colleges and universities are requiring that department chairmen be evaluated at stated intervals, such as every third, fifth, sixth, or tenth year. Some institutions rotate the chairmanship every five or six years.

After an evaluation of a department chairman has been made, what happens to the report? Except in those instances where the chairman is to be replaced, it would appear that the person being evaluated and his immediate superior would be the only persons who would benefit from sharing the detailed report. Some of the highlights of the report might be shared with members of the department where such sharing could result in improvement of the department. At any rate, prior to any evaluation, the persons to whom the report will be given should be determined.

HOW ARE EVALUATIONS MADE?

Up to this point various suggestions have been made about the evaluation of a department and its chairman. It is clear that there is no *one* way to do this. However, formal evaluations are being made and will continue to be made. The following steps are proposed as a logical procedure to be followed in appraising a department. The procedure is divided into three areas: preliminary steps, visitation, and preparation of the reports and their presentation to proper authorities.

Preliminary Steps before Any Evaluation.

1. The first step is the decision to evaluate. Someone has to decide that an evaluation should be made. As was pointed out earlier, the decision may be made by the head of the institution, by a dean or department head, by a committee, by an accrediting agency, or by the department itself.
2. After the decision to evaluate has been made, the reasons for the evaluation should be clearly stated. If the reasons for making the evaluation are to improve the quality of the program, then the study will take a different form than it will if the evaluation is for the purpose of considering the removal or replacement of the chairman.
3. The selection of a committee or team is the third step. The team chairman must be a person with stature and ability. Individual members of the teams must be persons with recognized competence and experience.
4. The committee may now develop the criteria to be used in this particular evaluation, or the criteria may have been developed over a period of time after much study and debate.
5. Self-evaluation should take place before the team visitation. This self-evaluation is done by a departmental committee or committees. This report should be completed and made available to team members for study before the visitation.

The Visitation. The visitation committee or team meets at a designated time and place for a preliminary discussion of procedures, for announcements, and for a general get-acquainted session. Following the first meeting, the committee meets with the chief administrator and his colleagues. Committee members are then usually paired off to secure information about facilities, libraries, records, faculty members, program philosophy, and the administrative structure. If only the administrator is being evaluated, the list of items for investigation will be limited. The committee makes it a point to talk with department heads, staff members, students, and other faculty members. Members of the committee also talk with deans, vice-presidents, and presidents. The committee attempts to gather information and to determine the educational climate and the philosophy of the department. Questionnaires, rating scales, and similar devices are used to compile as much information as possible.

The University of Kansas uses a questionnaire form for evaluating administrators and asks respondents to give written answers to the following questions:

1. Is the chairman effective in getting research facilities and outside funds for the department?
2. Is the chairman effective in obtaining university support?
3. Is he effective in recruiting new faculty?
4. Is he effective in his relations with the administration in the budget cycle?
5. Is he effective in creating a climate in which good teaching can take place?
6. Is he effective in stimulating research?
7. Is he effective in performing service functions for related departments?
8. Is he effective in carrying out departmental affairs and in maintaining departmental morale?
9. Is he effective in general departmental operations?
10. Are his personal relationships with members of the staff satisfactory? Does he have adequate communications with his staff?
11. Is he effective in his relationships with students in the department involving graduate student recruiting, local student relations, etc.?
12. Does the department obtain the maximum productivity for the staff and facilities available?
13. Is he effective in evaluating his staff?
14. Is he effective in planning for the future of the department?
15. Additional comments or suggestions. . . .[4]

The committee from Western Michigan University, using a different approach, developed a rating scale that attempts to evaluate performance of a department chairman on a five-point scale:[5]

DEPARTMENT HEAD RATING SCALE

Use the following list of job duties to rate the effectiveness (quality) of your department Head's performance over the past year. Please mark only those items which refer to tasks you have had an opportunity to judge yourself. Please be as objective as you can in your judgment of effectiveness.

List of Duties	**Effectiveness of Performance**				
	Very Good (1)	Good (2)	Avg. (3)	Fair (4)	Poor (5)
1. Represents Department to Administration	____	____	____	____	____
2. Represents Department and School to the public and various organizations	____	____	____	____	____
3. Obtains resources	____	____	____	____	____
4. Effectively allocates resources	____	____	____	____	____
5. Teaches	____	____	____	____	____
6. Consults with students	____	____	____	____	____
7. Is active professionally	____	____	____	____	____
8. Provides encouragement and direction to staff	____	____	____	____	____
9. Encourages professional growth of staff	____	____	____	____	____
10. Develops long-range plans to meet the needs of students and the objectives of the Department and the University	____	____	____	____	____
11. Implements Department and University policies	____	____	____	____	____
12. Provides leadership to meet the objectives of the Department	____	____	____	____	____
13. Communicates effectively with staff and other parts of the University	____	____	____	____	____
14. Recruits, recommends, promotes, and retains faculty in consultation with Department and Administration	____	____	____	____	____
15. Effectively assigns responsibility and authority to department members and committees	____	____	____	____	____
16. Sees that department members effectively fulfill assigned responsibilities	____	____	____	____	____

Western Michigan University lists three purposes of evaluating department chairmen:

1. To facilitate and accelerate the effectiveness of a department.

2. To affect the behavior of the department head.
3. To replace or remove a department head.

In addition to listing the purposes, their committee to develop procedures for the evaluation of department heads made eight recommendations as follows:

1. The department should be regarded as a core and unique unit within the university, and its head regarded primarily as a member of the department, chosen to facilitate its achievement.
2. Although it is the primary responsibility of the faculty to plan and evaluate the work of a department and its head, involvement at all levels of a university is encouraged.
3. Evaluation should be treated as a serious and difficult process. It should be periodically scrutinized to insure that it continues to facilitate university effectiveness.
4. Evaluation of a department head should be linked to, and an outgrowth of a serious and deliberate process of planning. In this process, the purposes and goals of the department and particular expectations for the department head could provide the basis for establishing criteria to be used in evaluation.
5. Information and interactions relevant to the planning should involve several levels within the university. Information on evaluative results should be of primary concern to the department head and to the evaluators. Evaluative results should not "bypass" the department head, except perhaps when the purpose is an appeal for replacement.
6. Criteria of evaluation need not be uniform across all departments. They should reflect the specific needs of a department at a given point in time.
7. The planning and evaluation process should be conducted so as to maximize opportunities for the department head and others to examine their interest in holding such a position. In some cases, trial periods may be indicated in lieu of replacement or resignation.
8. In cases where replacement is indicated, those seeking replacement should assume the burden of proof. A clearer university appeal process is needed for these situations.[6]

This is an excellent example of the considerations that can be developed by a good campus committee studying the problem of evaluation of department heads.

The foregoing instruments used by the University of Kansas and Western Michigan University illustrate attempts to measure department chairmen. Other institutions may use other methods. Rating scales and questionnaires are particularly valuable for use by committees from within the institution. They may be useful tools in any evaluation, but an evaluative committee must still use judgment in determining the final evaluation and making certain that the final appraisal is based upon facts that can be substantiated. Any evaluation based upon rumors, hearsay, and unsubstantiated evidence is unfair to the administrator or the department being evaluated. Irreparable damage may be done if unjust and unwarranted conclusions are drawn as a result of either faulty evidence or a biased committee.

When the evaluating committee is a team of experts from outside the college or university, even greater care must be taken to ensure that the bias of the individuals making the evaluation does not influence the final report. Unless the visiting team has certain guidelines to follow, it is entirely possible for the visitors to inject their own prejudices into the final report to the detriment of both the program and the department administration.

Before the visitation is completed, the committee findings should be discussed by the committee, and general agreement should be reached about the report.

Preparation of the Report. One or two members of the committee are usually appointed to write the report. Preliminary copies are then submitted to the committee members for their comments, additions, or revisions. The final document is then compiled after a consensus has been reached.

Following the final writing of the report, it should be submitted to the proper authorities. After the report has been presented, the work of the committee is finished except for answering questions that might be raised about the final evaluation.

The responsibility for implementing the findings of the report rests with those for whom the evaluation was undertaken.

SUMMARY

There are basically two types of evaluation of the administration of a department: informal and formal. Informal evaluations are constantly being made by the students, faculty, those in superior administrative positions, and by the various publics. Formal evaluations are made periodically. They may take the form of self-evaluation, evaluation by committees, either from within the college or university or from outside, or by accrediting agencies. State and regional accrediting agencies make evaluations as well as the National Council for the Accreditation of Teacher Education.

Administrators may be evaluated upon both personal qualities and administrative skills. Evaluation of a department should lead to improvement of the department and of the department chairman.

NOTES

[1] Van Miller, *The Public Administration of American School Systems* (New York: Macmillan Company, 1965), p. 474.

[2] Edgar M. Morphet, Roe L. Johns, and Theodore Reller, *Educational Organization and Administration, Concepts, Practices, and Issues,* 2d ed. (Englewood Cliffs, N.J.: Prentice-Hall, 1967), p. 533.

[3] Edward F. Voltmer and Arthur A. Esslinger, *The Organization and Administration of Physical Education,* 4th ed. (New York: Appleton-Century-Crofts, 1967).

[4] "Evaluation of the Department Chairman" Committee Report, University of Kansas, Lawrence, Kansas, 1971. Used by permission.

[5] "Evaluation of the Department Chairman" Committee Report, University of Western Michigan, Kalamazoo, Michigan, 1970. Used by permission.

[6] Ibid.

BIBLIOGRAPHY

Dimock, Marshall E. *The Executive in Action.* New York: Harper and Brothers, 1945.

Hagman, Harlan L. and Schwartz, Alfred. *Administrator in Profile for School Executives.* New York: Harper and Brothers, 1955.

Lane, Willard R.; Corwin, Ronald G.; and Manahan, William G. *Foundations of Educational Administration: A Behavioral Analysis.* New York: Macmillan Company, 1967.

Pfiffner, John M. and Sherwood, Frank P. *Administrative Organization.* 7th ed. Englewood Cliffs, N.J.: Prentice-Hall, 1966.

Van Fleet, James E. *Guide to Managing People.* West Nyack: Parken Publishing Co., 1968.

Wadia, Maneak S. *The Nature and Scope of Management.* Glenview: Scott, Foresman and Company, 1966.

Index